Dying to Live

Dying to Live
Lessons from Mark

John Churcher

Circle Books

Winchester, UK
Washington, USA

First published by Circle Books, 2012
Circle Books is an imprint of John Hunt Publishing Ltd., Laurel House, Station Approach,
Alresford, Hants, SO24 9JH, UK
office1@o-books.net
www.o-books.com

For distributor details and how to order please visit the 'Ordering' section on our website.

ISBN: 978-1-84694-715-5

A CIP catalogue record for this book is available from the British Library.

Design: David Kerby

Printed and bound in the United States of America by Edwards Brothers Malloy

Contents

Dedication

To Peter Brixey (1947-2010).
We disagreed over theology and politics yet he remained a close and loyal friend for over 50 years.

"If you accept uncritically and blindly, then it's clear that you don't have a lot of love for the truth. You have a love for what people tell you. Or it can be love for prevailing opinion. Sometimes we just fall in love with lies. Lies can generate some deep love. You can be addicted to lies and falsity as a way of dealing with life. You can fall for illusion, delusion, deception, and deceit."

Cornel West in *Hope on a Tightrope*, 2008

Acknowledgements

I am constantly grateful to a number of friends and mentors who have advised, cajoled but always remained constructively critical as I delved into the research and started writing the draft text of *Dying to Live*. Most notable has been Brian Wilson, who by his own admission was more of an academic *tormentor* than a mentor but without Brian this book would be little more than a set of rambling comments on Mark's Gospel.

Before you read further into this book there is a helpful and challenging comment that I received from Brian concerning my earlier book *Setting Jesus Free*. He made a reference to my repeated statements of 'following the Jesus Way' as having become "a sort of incantation... such mantras can soon seem to be empty rhetoric." I take seriously all critical comments and I hope to avoid some of the pitfalls and weaknesses that became apparent after that book was published. However, there are other mantras in this book, including another carried over from *Setting Jesus Free*:

> "Context, context, context,' and "You, the reader, must decide what is mythos, logos or Midrash!"

Rather than trying to express my experience of God as Perfect, Unconditional Love, all these experiential attributes can be summed up in a far better and more concise manner as 'Agape love'.

Albert Jewell wrote a critical but constructive review of *Setting Jesus Free* and I have taken note of his comments. I will, however, defend myself against one criticism: "the over-use of capital letters to designate preferred 'progressive' terms." I know what Albert is saying, but for me words and phrases such as 'Perfect Love', 'Agape Love', and 'Servanthood' need capital letters because they are not descriptors of actions for then they would require lower-case letters; but these are the names that I ascribe to whatever 'God' may be and therefore capital letters may be more appropriate. In using these words as proper nouns I am attempting to move the somewhat narrow and traditional view of 'God' as a 'Being out there' to something more relevant to the world in which we live: to a living Sacred Presence within and around every body. However, I will use lower case where appropriate! Albert has also commented upon the draft of *Dying to Live* and has influenced the development of my thinking.

Once again I am grateful to John Bedigan for helping me to keep the academic accessible to people too busy to spend much time on academia. Maria Larmer, Jairo Mejia and Richard Askew have asked many questions and commented extensively, shaping much of this book. Regular visitors to the permissiontospeak.org.uk forum have also challenged and influenced the development of my thinking, including Roger Baker, Philip Sudworth, Tony Buglass, John Paull and Seph Sayers. I have also been greatly encouraged by Jim Adams, and Joan and John Sigler.

I am particularly grateful to Keith Thompson, the staff and congregation at the First United Methodist Church in Boulder, Colorado for their welcome and hospitality during my short stay as a Theologian in Residence. This book was completed in the wonderful setting of Mountain Haven. It was also there in the solitude and unusually cold snowfall of May 2010 that Di Churcher spent much of the time going through the final draft. Betty Saunders suggested that this book would benefit from having a set of study questions – so I invited her to prepare them! My thanks to all of you.

Also I am grateful to you, the reader, that you are prepared to take the risk of thinking beyond the straightjackets of tradition and orthodoxy.

If you have any questions or comments after reading *Dying to Live* then please send these to me at www.permissiontospeak@rocketmail.com

John Churcher

Prologue

This book is a journey, not a destination. It is my continuing quest not in search of my integrity but to preserve it. It is never possible to define or even to redefine 'God' because whatever 'God' may be, 'God' is always more than any description of human language. What I and a great many other seekers after a deeper spirituality are redefining are our descriptions of the 'More Than God' that we experience in our time and place. Neither this nor my previous book *Setting Jesus Free* have been written to upset those who are content with the creeds and doctrines of the Christian Church. Both books are primarily for those who:

• remain in the Church by their fingertips, preferring the fellowship to the theology but wanting information to support and encourage them upon their own personal spiritual journeys;

• are part of that growing band of people who wish to follow the ethics and lifestyle of Jesus but for whom the Church has ceased to have relevance;

• are those with preaching and teaching responsibilities but who desire a new way of experiencing and describing their relationships with God and each other;

• are progressive Christians needing more information to help them declare what they believe and how their faith as a follower of the Jesus Way helps them live transformed lives (I long for progressive Christians to be confident and to speak out, not aggressively but with non-triumphalist zeal and enthusiasm).

At the end of reading *Setting Jesus Free* a reviewer sent me an adaptation of Sidney Carter's song *I danced in the morning…*

I danced on a Friday but the sky stayed blue
It's hard to know what is false and what is true
They buried my body and they thought I'd gone
You believed too much so I sent you John!
(Churcher)

Although this book follows on from *Setting Jesus Free* both can be read as freestanding. As you read this book, my advice to you is not to believe anything just because I explain what is true for me. Test it out and only in the lived experience will it become really true for you. There are three guiding principles underpinning this book:

• I cannot change history only interpret it so that it makes sense to me at this instant.

• I cannot know or control tomorrow, only anticipate it.

• It is in this moment alone when I have control over how I respond to others and how I live my life.

Many questions were put to me after the publication of *Setting Jesus Free*, and most seemed to involve questions about my, rather than the questioners', beliefs. But what is 'belief'? As far as I am concerned it has nothing to do with creeds, doctrines, dogma, or pleasing the *Old Man Above the Sky* kind of God with piety, prayer and good living. My 'belief' can be summed up as 'two sides of the same coin':

First, it is about the way in which Jesus lived, the way of agape love.

• This set him apart and made all the difference so that for those who wanted to see the God in him found it within the highest qualities of his humanity and vision. As I understand it, the life lived by Jesus was one of abundance – not material but of love, personal sacrifice and servant-hood. It was in Jesus the Special One that the indwelling God surfaced completely and uniquely.

Second, it is about the way in which I try to live:

• the more fully human I can become then the more I will experience the sacred. My belief is not about seeing life through rose-colored spectacles – it is not unrealistic. As I look at the daily news I know that there is a lack of humanity in all of us, and downright evil in some [see Appendix One for an example].

It is the Hindi word 'Namaste' or 'Namaskaram' (depending upon which part of India one references) that explains my understanding of the sacred. This word means, "May the God in me welcome and respect the God in you." It is this Namaste Spirit that was in Jesus that is in you and me.

A reader of *Setting Jesus Free* described me as a 'Christian Humanist' and I like that! However, I readily admit that there is a huge difference between my intentions and my accomplishments. But the ideal, as I see it, is the compassionate agape way of Jesus. Compassion should be the pathway into the sacred experience for all people. Such compassion will change the ordinary into the extraordinary of the ever-present sacred that is within us and about us.

My approach to the Bible

In *Setting Jesus Free* I highlighted the reasons for considering the Bible not to be God's Word in the sense that it was dictated letter by letter by God taking over writing hands and blank minds. It is my understanding and experience that the Bible is a human construct trying to explain each writer's experience of the sacred. But I emphasize again here that I approach the Gospel of Mark, as with all the Scriptures, with the understanding that it is record of a sacred encounter but described through the only things available to any of us, Mark included, the limitations of human words to describe the indescribable.

As I study the history of the Christian Church I see a distortion of what I understand to be the authentic message of the first century failed Jewish reformer of the Judaism of his day – Jesus of Nazareth. His life, witness and stories told constantly of what Funk (2002) calls "celebration" and a "radical inclusiveness".

Consequently there are many within the Church who perceive me as being a threat, but I can only maintain my integrity as both an ordained minister and as a follower of the Jesus Way of agape love if I challenge the belief, creeds, doctrines and dogma of the Church rather than go quietly into the night.

As I experience the 'churchianity' of the industrialized world I see gathering storm clouds and troubles ahead for its ever-dwindling Christian Church. It is essential that we all face the reality of the music that is coming to us from the world beyond the doors of the church: we need to listen and then to dance not just with new ways of expressing the Jesus experience but to Jesus rediscovered – the Jesus before the 4th century creeds 'got hold' of him!

Over recent years, Karen Armstrong has assisted my understanding of the nature of spirituality and the Bible in the books that she has authored. In *The Bible* Armstrong offers two helpful definitions to assist us as we approach the Scriptures, 'logos' and 'mythos'.

She defines 'logos' from the Greek meaning 'reason and an explanatory word'. In this context the 'logos' of God was associated with the Wisdom and Word of God that was responsible for Creation itself and which continues to speak with human beings at all times and in all places. Armstrong reminds us that it is in the preamble of John's Gospel that the assertion is made that God's Logos Word had been brought to life in Jesus of Nazareth.

Armstrong defines 'mythos' as another Greek word meaning 'any non-historical or fictional story' that was created to articulate the truth of an incident. A 'myth' is created so that individuals in all generations can recognize its authenticity within their own experiences. In this way, the experiential truth of the 'myth' happens not just once but also happens continually.

In her earlier book, *The Battle for God,* Armstrong highlights the differences between the ways in which pre-modern and post-modern worlds view history. The former had far less interest in the factuality of history than the latter. The pre-modern view of history was much more 'mythos', as an exploration of meaning, than as the factually correct 'logos' history recording that an event had actually happened. Armstrong says that to question the historical accuracy of the Bible record of, for example, Moses leading the people of the Exodus from Egypt into the Promised Land is to misunderstand the characteristics and objective of the story.

It is important to understand Armstrong's differentiation between 'logos', as being a factual report of an actual incident and 'mythos', a telling of a story packed with sacred meaning and truth if only we would look for it beyond the unscientific and the unbelievable elements of the story itself. My reference to and use of mythos and logos is based upon the line of reasoning that the writers of the Bible really did understand the difference between the two. If we confuse these – if we read what is essentially imaginative mythos as though it was factually true logos, we impair our understanding of the Scriptures.

In my experience the Bible is not a 'promise box' into which one may dig to find a verse to support one's own personal or corporate prejudices. For sure there will be a verse somewhere that, when taken out of context, can give an answer to a question for which a particular person seems to need 'Biblical authority' for its validation! Nor is the Bible a set of answers to every question that is posed. It is an open book in that there are contradictions that need to be treated as just that – contradictions because they reflect the context and the experiences of the writers at their own times and in their own particular places. The Bible was not written all at the same time. Nor did it come as a complete package from heaven!

One of the reviewers of *Setting Jesus Free*, Revd. Jairo Mejia was extremely complimentary but also highlighted the fact that in my list of resource books there was no mention of the work of Hans Küng. This sent me back to my bookshelves where I found an important work that meant nothing to me when I first read it but I now see how its thinking has influenced other writers who have subsequently enlightened my journey of faith [see Appendix Two]. Although the greatest contemporary influences upon my spiritual journey over the past 20 years or so have been Karen Armstrong, Marcus Borg, John Dominic Crossan, Elaine Pagels and John Shelby Spong, underpinning it all has been Rudolf Bultmann (1884-1976). Bultmann was concerned with demythologizing the Jesus supernatural stories, such as walking on the water and raising the dead, so that the message rather than the 'historicity' could speak afresh to those of us in the post-modern industrialized world for whom the supernatural is mainly found in movie theatres and novels. Along with Bultmann, my concern is to relate the mythos to the human condition so that it can shine a sacred light upon who and what we are as human beings who have yet to reach the fullness of humanity. However, I set the demythologizing of the Jesus supernatural stories within the Armstrong context of logos and mythos, leaving, you, the reader, to decide what is logos, mythos or Midrash.

I said a great deal about Midrash in *Setting Jesus Free* but I need to say more about it now. Midrash is a Hebrew word that means an interpretation of the Torah by digging out and shedding light on the meaning of the story. After all, the original purpose of the Torah was that of instruction or teaching. It was never intended to be an encumbrance but rather to be advice for life within the community of 'God's Chosen People'.

Midrash was developed through rabbinic argument, debate and dialogue and as a result was and remains greatly creative. It became a literary genre in its own right in that it was the way in which the ancient stories were explored, interpreted and explained for two purposes. According to Goulder's seminal book *Midrash and Lection in Matthew* (1974) Midrash was used [a] to edify and exhort the congregation, and [b] to reconcile the old teachings and ways with the new circumstances and experiences of the congregation. Isn't that what preachers and teachers do today without knowing or acknowledging that they, too, are using a form of Midrash?

Even in the time of Jesus, and for those Jews who followed him and were responsible for the writing of the pastoral letters and three of the Gospels in the Christian Testament, it was the major way in which the ancient stories were interrogated and applied to life.

Midrash can be divided into two basic types; the first is known as 'halakhah', meaning 'to walk'. This was the rabbinic interpretation and assistance on how to keep the Laws given by God and recorded in the Torah. The second form of Midrash is known as 'haggadah', which means 'to tell the story' in such a way that is accessible to all.

The Hebrew Testament, and subsequently the Christian Testament, always has sacred truth to offer to all times and in all places. Midrash is a legitimate rabbinic and inspired attempt to interpret the ancient eternal teachings so that they can be applied to contemporary situations using present-day and relevant language and thought forms. However, my understanding of Midrash convinces me that the Scriptures cannot be cherry-picked and applied unthinkingly to our contemporary times, circumstances and events.

We need to interpret and accept the Bible along with all its contradictions, and to learn to live with uncertainty and open-endedness. To do otherwise, to read the Scriptures literally, is to corrupt the text and to distort the Truth of the Eternal Spirit as it was interpreted by the writer within his [*sic*] experience described. The sooner we realize this and accept the truth of the confusion and contradiction, the sooner we can start to experience Jesus as he really was, so uniquely full of humanity that people experienced the fullness of the divine within him.

That is what the saints of the church have always been. We have seen this in people like Mother Theresa, Martin Luther King and Desmond Tutu, people so full of humanity and wisdom that we see the immense love and compassion that is God shining through their deeds and words.

It may not surprise you that I am often accused of failing to preach the Bible. I refute this accusation. I always preach the Bible but not in the way that literalists or fundamentalists seem to think is the only way to read and to interpret the Scriptures. I encourage people to love the Bible for what it really is: stories that interpret the struggle of human writers with the sacred Spirit, trying to understand the presence of the sacred within their own times and experiences. It is this human struggle with the sacred Spirit that makes the Bible divinely inspired. It is this same human struggle for understanding concerning the presence of the sacred in contemporary daily life that enables the Bible to be an inspiration of the divine for its readers in all times and all places.

We now come to a thorny issue concerning Jesus of Nazareth – was he a heretic or a prophet? In my understanding a prophet is a principal promoter of a movement or cause. From my studies of the Gospel stories, I conclude that Jesus was a leading advocate of a movement to unite and to reform the Judaism of his day, moving it away from 613 Laws to be rigidly adhered to, towards a way of life that was lived according to two principles: "Love God and love your neighbor as you love yourself."

This alone would have made Jesus into a prophet for those who followed him. It also made him a heretic to those Pharisees (later to be known as Rabbinic Judaism) and Sadducees (to disappear after the destruction of the Jerusalem Temple in 70 CE) who wanted to maintain all the Laws as they saw them and as they interpreted them – as much for political as for religious reasons. One person's prophet is indeed another person's heretic.

But the issue of heresy is a non-issue until either the power of the leadership or the comfort of the general public is challenged by the life and witness of the so-called prophet or heretic. Jesus could have grown old as a respected citizen – if he had only stuck to exorcisms, healings and wisdom teaching. But by the end of the first chapter of Mark's Gospel the outcome was inevitable.

Apart from those in his hometown of Nazareth, crowds of people accepted and welcomed Jesus as a wisdom teacher, exorcist and healer. In their experience and interpretation, Jesus was becoming the prophet who was advocating a new way of living God's will rather than living the way of the Pharisees and the Sadducees in their strict adherence to the Laws of Moses. But to the political and religious establishment – to the Jewish elite – Jesus was becoming an increasing threat and therefore was treated as a heretic who one way or another had to be stopped.

The rest of Mark's narrative unfolds the tragedy of what often happens when the prophet with right on his or her side challenges members of the elite who are exploiting their own power and might for either their own benefit or for the good of the people seen through the eyes of the powerful elites. And what of those within the Christian Church such as Bishop Spong who are prophets to some and heretics to others? They are prophets to progressive Christians who seek a new way of experiencing God, realizing that the Church cannot continue as it has been travelling for the past two millennia. But they are also heretics to hierarchies, fundamentalists and literalists afraid of what might happen if people, clergy and laity begin to openly ask difficult questions about the nature of belief and the future of the Church in this secular and post-modern world that is ours today.

However, I want to urge you not to be too hasty in judging who are today's heretics and prophets when it comes to interpreting the Scriptures and to challenging the ancient creeds and doctrines of a fading church. The history of the Christian religion is filled with those who were once thought to be heretics or dissenters who subsequently were welcomed as prophets. I think of the Augustinian monk Martin Luther who, by nailing his 97 Theses on the church door in Wittenburg in 1517, set in motion the great upheaval that created Protestantism out of the Catholic Church. To Protestants, Luther became a prophet but to the Catholic Church he was a heretic.

I think of Galileo, tried as a heretic by the Catholic Inquisition for statements that he made in 1632, saying that the Earth was not the center of the universe. Now Galileo is seen, not only as a prophet of science for supporting the earlier work of Copernicus, but also as the father of modern science by no less a person than Stephen Hawking.

"[4]Jesus said to them, "A prophet is not without honor except in his own town, among his relatives and in his own home." [Mark 6:4, New International Version]

As Spong reminds us, perhaps the main difference between heretics and prophets is only a matter of time?

Heresy or not, the purpose of this present book is to continue attempting to set Jesus free from the chains of two millennia of church power-broking and creedal over-spiritualizing of the one who was so full of humanity that people who wished to experience divinity did so in him. I am immensely grateful for the Church in general and for the Methodist Church in particular. But I am desperately concerned about the future of the institutional Church in much of the industrialized world. If we are honest it does not have a future if we continue to think in the limited language, sciences and theologies of the fourth century. The Church is in desperate need of a new reformation so that it may reinvent itself for our time. This book is not intended to further undermine the historic mainline churches or their dwindling numbers of the faithful in the industrialized world – traditional worship and creedal Christianity is doing that quite successfully without my help.

Dying to Live is intended to offer fresh ways of looking at the life and message of Jesus through Mark's Gospel, so that we who wish to follow his ways can make better sense of the Namaste Spirit that is present in all our lives today. This book is part of an ongoing attempt to breathe new life into the Church in the hope that it will slow the rate of decline by making the Jesus message relevant to the post-modern world (and in Europe, the post-Christian world) in which we live.

Knowing the context of the writing of the Scriptures is vital if we are to understand and interpret the stories so that they remain both within the Christian tradition and relevant to our contemporary world. Also we need to recognize a number of issues if we are to adequately interpret the Scriptures for our contemporary world. For example:

• The historical background to the writing of the Scriptures, such as two-thirds of the Hebrew Testament, were written either during or in the immediate aftermath of the devastating time of exile in Babylon, some six centuries before the birth of Jesus. The Hebrew Scriptures are predominantly stories of exile and return, and we should interpret them within this context.

• The importance of rabbinic argument in the exploration of the meaning of the ancient Torah's 613 laws that were not designed to restrict but to give freedom and spiritual abundance to the people. The importance of rabbinic Midrash – the retelling of ancient stories into new contexts that link Jesus with being the new Moses and the new Elijah.

• That not all the letters attributed to Paul in the Christian Testament were written by him or even in his lifetime, and that later 'Pauline' letters were written to undermine his radical social and religious beliefs.

• That Paul was dead before Mark wrote the first of the four Gospels in the Christian Testament.

• That Mark's Gospel is the record of the Apostle Peter's interpreted memories of his time with Jesus of Nazareth, and was the only Gospel written during a time of war between Palestine and Rome (64-73 CE).

• That Mark's Gospel was probably written in Greek but with Aramaic influences demonstrated in its geographic context and syntax suited more to the spoken languages of Palestine than to that of Rome. This may have reflected the influence of the Aramaic speaking and thinking Apostle Peter and his scribe and interpreter, Mark.

• That Matthew's Gospel is really Mark's Gospel and the Q source, along with amendments and additional stories to meet the needs of the Matthew community after the execution of Jesus, somewhere between 80 and 90 CE (it was known to Ignatius of Antioch in 110). The final version of Matthew's Gospel was written in Greek but there is scholarly discussion concerning the probability that the original version was written in the native language of Palestine.

• That Luke's Gospel, written in Greek, is Mark's Gospel, Matthew's Gospel and the Q source, with his own amendments and additions to reflect the fact that Luke was a Gentile convert to the teachings of Jesus. Although there is dispute as to the actual dating, most New Testament scholars date Luke between 85 and 90 CE.

• John's Gospel came later still, in the late 90s or very early 100s. Apart from the final nine chapters of John's Gospel, it was a written record of developing theology rather than history of the actual life of Jesus.

• That, in addition to these nine chapters, the history attributed to John in the Christian Testament can best be found in the three letters of John.

• That all the Gospels were written in times of brutal persecution by the Roman Empire and for the communities of Matthew and Luke, in a time of excommunication from their synagogues. For the Jews, this meant the devastation of the denial of their birthright.

• That not every saying attributed to Jesus in the Gospels was said by him, but reflected much more the interpretation of the stories and experiences of those who had been with Jesus.

• That much of the content of the Gospels is social commentary and should be read that way.

We do need to find new ways of experiencing and communicating the authentic pre-Constantine Jesus message to the world in which we live, free from creeds, doctrines, dogma and all the post-4th century words of the Church with which, I believe, Jesus of Nazareth would be extremely puzzled!

However, it is important, even for progressive Christians like me, not to reject the roots but to build upon these to guide and to inform a contemporary interpretation of the Jesus way. I have no intention of allowing my spiritual quest to grow out of or away from its Christian roots.

Dying to Live offers a challenge to all its readers to take the Bible seriously and to act upon what we find. This book is a further attempt at sharing contemporary Biblical scholarship with many who have no time for in-depth theological exploration but who want a faith that is intellectually satisfying and relevant to daily living. So there is one question that I hope every reader will constantly ask as you go through the pages: "What can I make of the sacred mythos so that it can be a living logos for me, lived out in my experience today and every day?"

As we set out together on this journey of discovery in the Gospel of Mark, I ask all readers: "Will you be romanced by and dance a new dance to the beautiful music of the Namaste Spirit shown so fully in Jesus of Nazareth? Will you allow yourself to be set free from the creeds and doctrines of the past that are now increasingly irrelevant in the present for many in the Church and for those beyond the church?"

Chapter One: Setting out on a Journey of Discovery

From the outset it is critically important to make two points. The first concerns Mark's Gospel itself. It is the memoirs of the Apostle Peter, told many times and eventually written down by Mark in the aftermath of the execution of both Peter and Paul. Over half of this Gospel records the last journey to Jerusalem and the events of that final week in the life of Jesus. Mark's Gospel does not present Jesus talking about himself as 'Son of God' but as one who is totally concerned with what it means to live the compassion that is the Kingdom of God in the present time.

The second point concerns this book, *Dying to Live*, in that all that follows is based on the premise that 'myth' is not a term of scholarly abuse but it is a positive statement that although an event may not be factually correct or even an historical occurrence, it is nonetheless full of creative sacred truth. Consequently, things do not have to be literally true for them to be intensely true in the experiences of the individuals concerned.

There are many ways in which Mark's Gospel can be interpreted and understood. In acknowledging that people interpret the Gospels in different ways I make known at this point that part of my personal perspective of interpreting the Gospels is within the context of a social justice agenda. I believe that social justice is the Namaste way of life. It was the driving force in the ministry and message of Jesus of Nazareth. This was put very clearly by West when he stated that God motivates any stance against injustice. He said that, if we are to take the cross seriously, social justice is an echo of God's voice (2008, page 169).

What now follows in the rest of this chapter is an overview of some of the different ways of reading and interpreting the Gospels. It deals with varying scholarly approaches that suggest alternative reasons as to why Mark's Gospel was written. For example:

- To fit into a developing Jewish Christian liturgy.

- As a 'narrative' or a 'myth-novel' reflecting the social context of 7th decade Rome.

- As an interesting biographical story of Jesus told by the Apostle Peter and written by Mark following the execution of his mentor, Peter.

- As interpreted history in which Mark used a well-established literary genre to select his subject matter and then he exaggerated it to emphasize the significance of what he considered to be a particularly important event.

This chapter also considers the way in which Matthew and then Luke plagiarized the Gospel of Mark and added their own stories to meet the developing needs and questions of their own communities. It also looks at the way in which 'we' can interpret the Bible through 21st century experiences and not the experiences of the original writers or later commentators. I suggest that we need to think through the extent to which our reading of a Bible story is our interpretation of the writer's interpretation of his own experiences – and doubtless the two are not the same!

This chapter is concluded with consideration of how the creeds and doctrines of the Church have come about.

I suggest to readers who have little time to devote to this background information that you go straight to Chapter Two. However, for those who have the time to consider why I am convinced that the Gospels were not written in the way that we usually read them, then do continue reading through the rest of this chapter. I am sure that your time will not be wasted!

Detailed background material

One can read the Gospel in its simplest way – taken at face value and read as a chronologically and geographically accurate record of the ministry, life and death of Jesus of Nazareth. In this approach there is no need to be concerned with the context of the writing of the Gospel and, because it is 'the Word of God', it can be trusted to be true in all respects. This is the way in which Mark's Gospel has been read and interpreted for centuries.

Yet another way in which one can approach this Gospel is by following the scholarship of Goulder and Spong. Both have studied the 5th century manuscript of Mark's Gospel, entitled the *Codex Alexandrinus*. This *Codex* has 49 sections, each one numbered and titled. Goulder and Spong have concluded that Mark's Gospel is a succession of Sabbath readings linked directly to the Jewish liturgical lectionary cycle.

To Goulder and Spong, the subject matter of Mark's Gospel was neither an accurate chronological record of the adult life and death of Jesus, nor was it a random selection of events remembered from the life of Jesus. If Goulder and Spong are correct then the Peter/Mark stories were selected and determined by the worship needs of their early Jewish-Christian community as it met in the Jewish synagogue alongside those Jews who rejected the Messianic claims assigned to Jesus by early Jewish Christian leaders.

For example, Goulder and Spong suggest that by placing Mark 16, the Passion story of Jesus, to be read on the equivalent of our Easter Sunday, the rest of the *Codex Alexandrinus* sections fit into 49 weeks of the Jewish liturgy. Although reading Mark's Gospel as a Jewish Christian liturgy leaves approximately one-third of the Jewish Sabbath cycle without comparable content, it is possible to identify which part of Mark applies to which part of the Jewish cycle.

Goulder offers a further example in that the Jewish liturgical cycle included the book of Deuteronomy that was read over twelve Sabbaths. Careful comparison between Deuteronomy and Mark 10-

12 (the journey of Jesus and his disciples from Galilee to Jerusalem) demonstrates a Midrashic mirror image at work. Examples include teaching on humility; schism within the fellowship; rules governing marriage and divorce; nurturing of children; affluence and possessions. Then in Mark 13 Jesus speaks of the imminent arrival of the Messiah and the end times of this world. This would have been the Jewish Christian reading for the exact Jewish Sabbath dealing with the time when the 'old' gave way to the 'new'.

When considering why the later Gospel of Matthew is longer than Mark's, Spong suggests that additional stories were included to complete the gaps between Mark and the Jewish lectionary Sabbath cycle. It should be noted that most of the additional material in Matthew's Gospel (and then copied by Luke) comes either side of Mark's account: the genealogy and the birth stories of Jesus, and the period post-Easter to Pentecost. The *Codex Alexandrinus* edition of Matthew's Gospel contains 69 named sections so there is sufficient material to mirror and supplement the entire Jewish Sabbath cycle. Matthew's Gospel can also be broken into 5 distinctive blocks of teaching that follow and would have been read during the five great Jewish liturgical festivals.

Goulder and Spong also state that this Christian Gospel/Jewish liturgical Sabbath and Festival lectionary approach is in fact Midrash at work. An example is that of the birth story of Jesus – it is the Midrash of the birth and babyhood of Moses. In this way of the Midrashim, the Synoptic Gospel writers took relevant stories from the Hebrew Testament and rewrote these into the Jesus context. As such, the Midrash of the Synoptic Gospel writers was never intended to be a historically factual record of what Jesus said and did. Doubtless the Gospels were written by taking 'logos' (factual events remembered by the Apostle Peter) and building the mythos (not to be read literally but nonetheless full of sacred truth) upon it to explain the ongoing Jesus experiences of the writers and their respective communities decades after the execution of Jesus.

Part of me would like to think that Mark's Gospel, being the nearest in our canon of Scripture to the events recorded, was written more or less in chronological order. However, whether or not Goulder and Spong are correct, Mark's Gospel increasingly seems to me to be a work of creativity in which Mark took the 'Jesus stories' of Peter and reordered them into narrative sections to make the memories of Jesus more accessible and relevant to his community readers and listeners. As such, they probably do not represent an accurate chronological development of the ministry of Jesus. That is why I constantly write such as "according to the narrative" or "Mark now suggests" and similar indicators to remind the reader that I am aware of the rearranged narrative.

However, the way in which I read and interpret the Gospel of Mark is to see it primarily as a 'narrative' or a 'myth-novel' written within the social context of 7th decade Rome, to encourage the faithful during times of persecution and execution. The more I read and study this Gospel, and the more that I can clear my mind of the gentile 'Gospel' interpretation and spin placed upon Mark since the turn of the first century, the more I can read it as an interesting biographical story of Jesus explored through the memories and oral stories told by the Apostle Peter.

Furthermore, the Gospel of Mark was a compilation of stories originally written as continuous text without any chapters, paragraphs or numbered verses. It was not until the 13th century CE that Stephen Langton, Archbishop of Canterbury, developed the chapter structure that we have today. The first division of chapters into verses had to wait another two centuries before Robert Estienne did this.

Also in this context it is important to cite the classical scholar, Francis Macdonald Cornford, Fellow of Trinity, Cambridge. I am grateful to Brian Wilson for offering guidance on the work of Cornford. Cornford studied the basic principles and myths that underpinned classical Greece. Among his publications was *Thucydides Mythistoricus* (1907) in which Cornford considered the work of the Greek historian Thucydides (460 BCE-395 BCE) and his exploration of the history of the 5th century BCE. Thucydides interpreted history by selecting his subject matter and then exaggerated it to emphasize the significance of a particular historical event.

'Mythistoricus' is a Cornford adjective/adjectival noun that I interpret as 'myth-history' and as such consider it to be appropriate in our exploration of the nature and purpose of the Christian Testament's four Gospels. Increasingly I find that *Mythistoricus* is important when considering the way in which Mark interpreted the oral Jesus stories told him by the Apostle Peter: Mark embellished and rearranged these in a similar way to that in which Thucydides had explored his historical stories.

Matthew, followed by Luke and then John all continued a similar 'myth-history' approach. Indeed, when I read John's Gospel I see it even more as written in the genre of that used by Thucydides. However, far from removing the sacred truth from Jesus by suggesting that the Gospels were increasingly 'myth-history', I am convinced that such an approach to the Gospels adds to my experiences and descriptions of the sacred truth of 'God' within us and about us, met in Jesus.

Although Mark's Gospel was written specifically for his community at that time, in my opinion each generation needs to come afresh and to reinterpret the Scriptures for the contemporary times of the reader and not just those of the writer. Again, it is wrong to interpret the Scriptures as anything other than human creations, resulting from the struggles of the writers with the eternal Namaste Spirit to try to understand what their vision and experience of 'God' was doing in their time and place. It is the same Namaste Spirit with whom we struggle to interpret the Scriptures for ourselves today.

Contemporary biblical scholarship is now more or less in agreement that the history-interpreted stories of Peter, recorded in Mark, were subsequently followed by Matthew, then Luke and finally by John. All were written, Gospel on Gospel, with an increasing number of explanatory stories and truth-packed myths about the person and work of Jesus of Nazareth, along with the obvious comment that both Hebrew and Christian Testaments are confusing and both contain a great many contradictions. It seems to me that none of the Gospels were written to be selected, subsequently, for a Canon of Christian Scripture!

So what have all these conflicting statements, contradictions and chronological discrepancies got to do with being a Christian in the 21st century? In my opinion they are fundamental to the survival of both the Christian faith and the Christian Church in our industrialized world. We need to take the Gospels for what they are – stories about Jesus, adapted for particular people and their circumstances. If we can do this then contradictions and confusions become irrelevant. The Church is not infallible. The Gospel writers were not infallible. The Bible as a whole is not infallible.

When we read and study the Bible we always need to go beyond the stories themselves. I cannot emphasize enough that to read the Bible primarily as mythos takes nothing away from its sacredness and means that it never had to be 100% historically true for it to be always true in personal experience.

In our post-modern and post-Christian world it is not important to count up how many of the events and personalities in, for example, the birth or resurrection stories of Jesus we think are historically real. But it is vitally important for us and for the future of the Christian Church that we come to these Gospel stories knowing that they were written in their own particular ways, not because they were necessarily historically true but because they tell of the experiences of the sacred Namaste Spirit met in Jesus by the authors of the Mark, Matthew, Luke and John Gospels decades after the execution of Jesus.

What we need to do is to seek the sacred meaning beyond the logos upon which these stories may or may not have been based. The most important search is within and beyond the creative mythos of the stories of the Scriptures so that our everyday lives in this broken and incomplete world are invigorated: so that our lives will be changed by the presence of the sacred within and about each one of us.

The mantra: "Context, context, context"

One of the shortcomings of biblical interpretation is that many Christians often content themselves with reading the narrative at face value on the assumption that the text is factually true: for example, the world was created in six days because the Bible says so. Perhaps this thinking is part of the reason why the Christian Church in Britain is losing an average 2000 members every week? Such assertions of simple faith make little sense to the majority in our developing multi-choice, multi-faith, and multi-scientific world.

We need to read and to interpret both the Hebrew and Christian Testaments in a far wider context than is the usual within most of our church preaching and Bible study groups. [See Appendix Three for additional relevant background information on the Gospels of Matthew and Luke.]

The Bible is factual history only when it comes to verifiable items such as dates of exile and return; names of kings and prophets; Jesus of Nazareth existed and had a band of followers long after his execution. As soon as attempts are made to give reasons for these verifiable items, the Bible ceases to be factual history.

Explained history is never what really happened. History beyond the verifiable facts is always an interpretation of stories and experiences because we can never read ourselves into the thought processes of the original writer or into the actual experiences of the people involved in the factual history explored and explained.

There is also the added dimension that will impact upon any interrogation of the past: 'we' interpret history through 21st century experiences and not the experiences of the original writers. We need, therefore, to think through the extent to which our reading of a Bible story is our interpretation of the writer's interpretation of his own contemporary events or past stories of faith. To do this we need to consider the extent to which actual historical events were enhanced in their telling and recording by added dimensions of meaning by the writers, for their immediate communities.

When reading the Scriptures I see, time and time again, accounts of what may have been based upon history becoming myth as new layers of interpretation and understanding were placed upon the ancient stories. But once again, in the biblical context, 'myth' does not mean historically 'untrue' but rather a higher truth based upon the sacred experiences of the writers.

All this needs to be kept in mind as we attempt to seriously interrogate the Christian Testament to understand what the writers were really saying. Only in this way can we interpret those scriptures with a new meaning and relevance for life today. Context, context, context – this is my mantra!

This is also where I adapt what is known as the Wesleyan Quadrilateral as a methodology [a] to guide my understanding of what it means to be a follower of the Jesus Way today, and [b] to inform my contemporary theological reflection.

- The first is scripture itself: to be read, as best we can, within the contexts of both [i] the writings themselves and [ii] the intentions of the writers.

- The second is tradition: spanning two millennia of the Christian church but not locked into such as post-Constantine or pre-Enlightenment thinking, creeds and doctrines.

- The third is reason: post-Enlightenment rational thinking and sensible interpretation of the Scriptures based upon contemporary biblical scholarship, social and scientific developments, etc.

- The fourth is experience: both a personal and a communal faith pilgrimage centered on the historical Jesus rather than the Jesus of the creeds and doctrines of the Church.

I love the Church and I am deeply concerned for its future. This is why I preach and write in the way that I do. In public worship I still reference the doctrines of the Methodist Church because, for example, Father, Son and Holy Spirit are the traditional words employed to describe the experiences of the indescribable 'God' – but 'God' is more than this and Trinitarian doctrine needs to be set within the greater context of the 'More Than God'. Both Judaism and Christianity have survived against all the odds by continually reinventing themselves. We in the Christian Church need to do the same again now. If we fail to develop our thinking and our theology then the Church as we know it will surely die.

I further suggest that most people outside the Church today treat, for example, the Christmas and Epiphany stories as 'once upon a time' stories and as such also go on to reject all the rest of the Jesus story presented through the creeds and doctrines of the Church. However, their 'once upon a time' approach to the Christmas and Epiphany stories may be closer to the truth and to the original intention of the Gospel writers than the literalism of the creeds and doctrines created down the centuries by the Church!

For example, I am convinced that the Matthew story of the magi never happened in history but it should always happen in our experience. It is a mythos that can be lived out by us as logos – a creative story made real in our experience today. Although the author of the Gospel of Matthew was not writing factual history, we are invited by the same sacred Namaste Spirit at work in the writing of the Gospel of Matthew to ask what the story of the wise men might have to say to us today. But you must answer that question for yourself!

As with much of the Scriptures, the story of the magi does not have to be historically true for it to be always true in our daily lives and experiences. The power of the story of the wise men, the wandering star and the slaughter of the innocents is not in its historical accuracy but in our struggle with the sacred Namaste Spirit to understand the story – to understand the sacred mythos – to make it a daily-lived experience as we struggle to come to terms with the findings of such as Goldstone's Report on the Israeli invasion of Gaza in early 2009. Just how do we apply the magi mythos of Jew and Gentile (Jew and Arab) accepted equally by the One God of All, living peacefully side by side, when there is a continuing slaughter of innocents on both sides?

Unless our Christian stories impact upon the way in which we are both proactive and reactive to personal, communal, national and international events then what use is it to have a belief in any God? Faith without actions for the common good, and without offering hope and an abundance of life (not possessions!) to all, is dead faith. It may be little more than a crutch to support our own prejudices, closed minds and lack of actions.

As an example, on 22nd March 2010 I felt utter shame that the Mayor of Jerusalem was in London to address a meeting at Chatham House. His speech concerned his vision for the future of Jerusalem as a city for the whole world, when he is part of the system that is ethnically cleansing East Jerusalem and maintaining Gaza as the largest prison in the world. As I stood there among the 200 or so protesters I felt a real sense that the central message of Jesus was that of justice. I was among the usual Arabs, Muslims, peace activists, Quakers and to my utter joy, a dozen members of 'Jews United Against Zionism'. Orthodox Jews were waving Palestinian flags and displaying banners with messages such as 'Judaism rejects the Zionist State and condemns its atrocities' and 'Zionism and Judaism are extreme opposites'. There was I, a British Methodist minister whose own commitment to justice and peace in the Middle East was summed up in those Jewish banners.

There is another example much closer to home for those of us in the industrialized world: our profligate and cavalier attitude towards the climate and Creation is coming back to haunt us. But as always, the saddest part is that it is the poorest of the world that will be hit first. These are the people who have not caused global climate change but these will suffer the most. If there is ever a lesson from history, it is that such deprivation and innocent suffering is a breeding ground for religious fanatics and political extremists. Coming to the Bible with an open questioning mind so that we are honest about our Scriptures is a key that may unlock the door to saving the Church in the age in which we live. Coming to all Creation with humanity in our hearts, minds and actions may just save human kind and this planet for the generations still to come.

'With hindsight'

But I turn again to the Gospel of Mark where there is another major difference of which we need to be aware. This time it is between seeing the Gospel of Mark for what it was originally intended to have been, Peter's interpreted memories set within a social commentary of the life and the times of the early Christian community in Rome, and for what it has become, part of a 'with hindsight' theologically interpretative over-spiritualizing of the life of Jesus by the Christian Church. This began with the Apostle Paul and was followed by Matthew, Luke and John. This process continued right through to the 4th century bloodletting, infighting and excommunications that accompanied the Church Councils and the writing of creeds such as Nicaea (325 CE) and the development of doctrines such as Trinitarianism at Constantinople (381 CE).

As I study the Christian Testament I find an increasing gentile rejection of the Jewish background, moving eventually to a situation in which Christianity removed itself almost completely from its original Jewish roots. For example, I doubt that some of the titles given to Caesar Augustus and then to Jesus after his execution (e.g. Son of God; Prince of Peace; Savior of the World) would have been recognized by Jesus as applicable to himself. Another example: ignoring the mythos of demons recognizing Jesus as the Son of God, there are just five stories in the synoptic Gospels of Mark, Matthew and Luke where people make such a profession:

- The healing of the demon-possessed man in the region of Gerasene who made the first recognition of deity: 6When he saw

Jesus from a distance, he ran and fell on his knees in front of him. [7]He shouted at the top of his voice, "What do you want with me, Jesus, Son of the Most High God? In God's name don't torture me!" [Mark 5:6-7 (New International Version) also told in Matthew 5:7 and Luke 8:28.]

[39]And when the centurion, who stood there in front of Jesus, saw how he died, he said, "Surely this man was the Son of God!" [Mark 15:39 (New International Version) and Matthew 27:54]

• In the mythos of Jesus walking on the stormy waters to the small boat, and then calming the waves, we find Matthew's first recognition of deity: [32] And when they climbed into the boat, the wind died down. [33] Then those who were in the boat worshiped him, saying, "Truly you are the Son of God." [Matthew 14:32-33 (New International Version)]

• Peter's confession that Jesus was the Christ: [15]"But what about you?" he asked. "Who do you say I am?" [16]Simon Peter answered, "You are the Messiah, the Son of the living God." [17]Jesus replied, "Blessed are you, Simon son of Jonah, for this was not revealed to you by flesh and blood, but by my Father in heaven. [Matthew 16:15-17 (New International Version)]

• The events following the mythos of the physical resurrection of Jesus: [54]When the centurion and those with him who were guarding Jesus saw the earthquake and all that had happened, they were terrified, and exclaimed, "Surely he was the Son of God!" [Matthew 27:54 (New International Version)]

There are alternative versions of these same stories in the other Gospels in which the profession of Jesus as the Son of God is not made. I conclude that even in the five 'Son of God' examples given, these may well have been written into the mouths of Jesus followers as the theology of the Gospel writers developed in the latter years of the first century CE.

Another important parallel that needs to be recognized is that the title 'Son of Man' is used much more prolifically in the Christian Testament. Mark uses it 13 times; Matthew 29 times; Luke 25 times; John 12 times; the rest of the Christian Testament just twice. So the Gospel theme was not really Son of God but rather Son of Man. This is important as the writing of the Christian Testament was by Jews (with the exception of the Gentile Luke who was, nevertheless, steeped in Judaism) and Judaism understands 'Son of Man' as a phrase that draws attention to the differences between God and human beings. Note, it did not mean "God from God" or "God's Only Begotten Son".

In the mythos stories of God's communications with the prophet Ezekiel, the term 'Son of Man' is used and applied to Ezekiel some 90 times to emphasize that Ezekiel was not 'God' or the 'Son of God' or 'Messiah' but that he was the one fit person at that time to be God's prophetic voice to the people. The Jews who were following Jesus in the first century CE were schooled in Judaism and its understanding of what 'Son of Man' actually represented: Jesus was a prophet in the great line of Ezekiel et al, the one fit to be God's prophetic voice in their time. The theology developed from 'Son of Man' into 'Son of God' over the following two centuries. Landmark decision makers in this process were:

• Justin Martyr (second century) developed the idea of Jesus as the Logos.

• Irenaeus (second century) defended traditional Christianity, even at that early stage in its development, from the Gnostics.

• Tertullian (early third century priest) was instrumental in developing Christology and the doctrine of the Trinity.

• Fourth century developments and arguments were led by men

such as Arius, Athanasius, Basil of Caesarea, Gregory of Nazianzus and Gregory of Nyssa.

I am convinced that the creeds and doctrines of the fourth century Christian Church, whether they were those of the Eastern or the Western Church would have been unrecognized by the historical Jewish Jesus who had walked on this earth. Once again I ask whether or not that makes me a heretic? Even today, in the Christianity of the West we place great emphasis upon substitutionary atonement in which Jesus died and took our sins upon himself. There is no such concern for this within the Eastern Church. Instead, the great emphasis there is upon the joy and wonder of the Incarnation, that God should come in the flesh of a human being.

In the next chapter we begin to consider the Christian Testament in general and the Gospels in particular as being written as social commentary with a developing theology rather than as a complete theology and Christology at the time of their writing.

Chapter Two: Mark's Gospel as Social Commentary

It is important to underline the fact that Mark's Gospel has neither a birth or resurrection story of Jesus. Notice that the ending of the earliest versions of this Gospel have nothing beyond the visit of Mary Magdalene, Salome and Mary the mother of James to the tomb of Jesus early on the Sunday morning that Christians celebrate as Easter Day. On the strength of this Gospel record, where Jesus came from and where he reputedly went after his execution really were not the concerns of Peter or Mark.

In a similar way, the Apostle Paul's authentic letters that were written before any of our Gospels were written are not in the least bit concerned with how Jesus was born, and little interested in what he did while going about his life and ministry on earth. What was important to Paul was how the followers of the Jesus Way lived out the Jesus message in their own time and place. [See Appendix Four for more detail concerning the authentic letters attributed to Paul.]

Peter/Mark's Gospel was the least theological of the Gospels and the nearest that we can get to the actual historic events concerning Jesus of Nazareth. But even in saying that, Peter's memories of the life and death of Jesus were not 100% factual history. I repeat that they were Peter's memories of his time with Jesus and then filtered through his experiences in the three decades beyond the execution of Jesus. As such, Mark's Gospel is history remembered and then history interpreted by Peter. Mark then creatively adapted it. It was never intended to be an accurate, beyond doubt, factual history of the life and times of Jesus.

However, to understand Mark perhaps we have first to know something about the Apostle Peter. The general acceptance is that Peter was originally named Simon but Jesus changed this to Peter, meaning 'the rock'. From the Gospel stories, it can be assumed that Peter was a fisherman by trade, living in Capernaum. He was often impetuous, acting before thinking [Mark 9:4-6] although he is credited with having the spiritual insight to be the first disciple to recognize Jesus as the Messiah [Mark 8:27-30]. Many Christians interpret this as meaning Peter was 'the rock' upon which the Church has been built, while other Christians reject this and proclaim that it was Peter's affirmation of Jesus upon which the Church was built. Peter is also remembered as one who, during his travels with Jesus, promised much but delivered little. Even when Jesus was arrested in Gethsemane, rather than acting in the way of passive resistance that marked the ministry of Jesus, Peter is reputed to have reverted to the old ways of living and dying by the sword [John 18:9-11].

Notice, however, in the Gethsemane story recorded in both Mark 14:46 and Matthew 26:50 it is a companion rather than specifically Peter who is mentioned as having the sword. Perhaps Mark's Gospel records the sword wielder as being a 'companion' of Jesus rather than naming Peter specifically because Mark is protecting his colleague and friend, Peter, from accusations of having got even this wrong? Or, perhaps, it really was an unnamed companion rather than Peter, but the author of John's Gospel wanted to put the boot (if not the sword!) into Peter, especially as the context of the Letters of John seems to me to be warnings against defecting from John's communities to the rival communities that followed the teaching and leadership of either Peter or Mary Magdalene? [See Appendix Five for more information concerning the Letters of John.] Perhaps it was enough for Mark to record Peter's great betrayal in the courtyard of the High Priest that he did not want to put the Gethsemane sword into Peter's hand as well!

But Peter was much more than all of that. We remember him as the one who, after the execution of Jesus, took charge on the day of Pentecost and preached with authority and power. Although this is often referred to as the Baptism in the Holy Spirit, was this the second coming of the Jesus Spirit? I ask this because in John's Gospel, Chapter 20, the 'baptism' in the Spirit occurred on Easter Sunday in the upper room:

> [19]On the evening of that first day of the week, when the disciples were together, with the doors locked for fear of the Jewish leaders, Jesus came and stood among them and said, "Peace be with you!" [20] After he said this, he showed them his hands and side. The disciples were overjoyed when they saw the Lord. [21]Again Jesus said, "Peace be with you! As the Father has sent me, I am sending you." [22]And with that he breathed on them and said, "Receive the Holy Spirit. [23]If you forgive anyone's sins, their sins are forgiven; if you do not forgive them, they are not forgiven." [John 20:19-23 (New International Version)]

Peter also started his leadership role still maintaining the exclusivism of the Jews in as much as Yahweh God was concerned primarily with Jews – not with gentiles. It took the request of the gentile Cornelius and an accompanying vision that enlightened Peter to the truth of what Jesus had found as a result of the encounter with the Syro-Phoenician woman: that Yahweh God was concerned with all people without favoritism or prejudice [Acts 10:1–23].

Often remembered is Peter's growing reputation and courage shown in the incident in which he was imprisoned by King Herod but then miraculously freed [Acts 12:1-19]. It is also commonly accepted that Peter spent his later years in Rome where he was martyred in 64 or 65 CE during the Nero-inspired persecution.

If one opts for the earlier 65-68 CE date of writing, then Mark's Gospel was written during Emperor Nero's bloody persecution of synagogue members, including both Jew and gentile followers of the Jesus Way, that resulted in the executions of both the Apostles Paul and Peter. If one opts for the post-70 writing of Mark then it was written during or in the immediate aftermath of the rebellion and war in Palestine as the Jews attempted to throw off the shackles of Rome. This war was disastrous and not only was the Jerusalem Temple destroyed but the Sadducees and their Temple Cult was destroyed with it.

Marcus Borg says that this makes Mark our only wartime (as opposed to occupation) Gospel. War and persecution form the context of the writing of Mark's Gospel and, again, it should be read in that way. As such, I cannot emphasize enough that Mark was writing in a time of brutal Roman Imperial military power, exploitation and, from time to time, bloody persecution. In addition to the executions of Peter and Paul, others of the sisters and brothers were being thrown to the lions and the gladiators or burned like candles.

Mark's encouragement to the people is pragmatic social commentary and advice: do not respond to violence and intimidation in the ways of the wisdom of the world or in the ways in which others may expect you to answer back. According to Mark, the ideal (and I stress the ideal) response is that of peaceful passive resistance: "Give to Caesar what is Caesar's and to God what is God's" comes readily to mind! Such logos social commentary then became part of the mythos of early theology for Christians in Rome by associating such responses as being the way of the Kingdom of God.

For a short time we now need to step back even further in years to Julius Caesar. He had been deified in 42 BCE, two years after his assassination. Subsequently his adoptive heir, Octavius (later to be renamed Augustus) fought a Civil War against his earlier ally, Mark Anthony. Along with Cleopatra, Mark Anthony's fleet was defeated on 2 September 31 BCE on the Ionian Sea. The battle was fought off the Greek coast near the Roman colony of Actium. There was an ancient Temple to Apollo at Actium and to celebrate the victory of Octavius Augustus additional inscriptions were made there in honor of the victor who not only brought peace to the Roman Republic but also signaled the beginning of the Roman Empire.

According to Borg and Crossan, by putting these together with other inscriptions in Rome, Antioch, Ankara and on temples throughout the Roman Empire, Octavius Augustus was declared (self-declared in some cases!) as "Divine; Son of God; God, God from God, Lord, Redeemer and Savior of the World". This was a theme taken up within the century and applied by his followers to Jesus of Nazareth – in itself a hugely political as well as religious statement! Two years after his death the Roman Senate, in 14 CE, officially deified Augustus as 'son of a god'. This was not the same as the Jewish belief concerning the Son of the only real God: all other gods were false and imaginary. However, at that time, for any person or group to claim that Jesus was God and all other gods were false was a direct assault upon the Roman Emperor and doubtless would have been considered a capital offence.

It is within this political context that I suggest that Mark's Gospel should be studied with an eye upon coded messages that reflected the social conditions of the time: to be openly critical of Rome was tantamount to signing one's own death warrant. However, to conceal the logos within the mythos of coded stories was a way in which both writer and reader might find some protection. It was the mythos that later, mistakenly, became interpreted as logos theology.

An example of this is an amazing story in Mark 5. Here we read of Jesus being confronted by a Jewish man who was possessed with an evil spirit. He had been consigned to the cemetery where he was bound and chained. But he was so strong he kept breaking his bonds and now Mark has him meeting Jesus on the seashore. There is a plea from the mad man that Jesus would not torture him any further. According to the Contemporary English Version, Jesus asked him his name and the man replied, "My name is Lots, because I have lots of evil spirits!" But the New International Version has the man answer, "My name is Legion, because we are many!"

We need to think carefully about this. Mark was writing to Jewish and gentile followers of Jesus at a time of persecution by Rome. By casting out the evil spirits Mark shows that Jesus has power over the Legion of evil spirits that possessed and tormented this Jewish man. When one begins to read the Christian Testament, not as accurate logos history but as allegory and metaphor; as mythos based upon logos, perhaps a new vision of Jesus and of the life of the early communities of his followers begins to emerge and excite us afresh about the Bible? The occupying Roman soldiers were organized into Legions. The coded message to the followers of Jesus might have been that even though they suffered greatly under the brutality of the Legions of Rome, by standing fast the Jesus Spirit would overcome even the power of Rome.

What we can be sure about is that faithful Jews could not have owned the pigs into which Jesus cast the evil spirits. Judaism and pigs just do not mix! As I mentioned in *Setting Jesus Free* [pages 63-65], if this event really happened in logos history then Jesus was an economic vandal. His action cleansed the Jewish mad man but destroyed the livelihood of the non-Jews who owned and looked after the pigs. At this stage in the ministry of Jesus, non-Jews were still no better than dogs and their livestock could be dispensed with.

Or is this yet another coded mythos message of Mark in which Jesus the Jew was representative of the Jewish cause and demand for self-determination and freedom from Roman occupation? One day the 'Legion of evil spirits' would be destroyed and, as a consequence, the economic power of Rome would be broken. But to say this openly and not under the shadow of creative mythos storytelling would surely have had Mark arrested, tried and executed for insurrection. In my opinion, Mark's narrative of the life and death of Jesus was written in such a way that the growing possibility and awareness of Jesus as God could be discussed without alerting the powers of the State to the truth being experienced and the message being conveyed concerning Jesus. Mark's Gospel is possibly full of coded messages reflecting the social conditions of the time – a narrative and social commentary not unlike the works of Charles Dickens almost two millennia later?

The rest of this chapter considers Peter's developing theology, the hierarchy of the Christian communities in the mid to late decades of the first century, and the Pharisaic proclamation of holiness by separation. Once again I suggest to readers who have little time to devote to this additional information that you go straight to the next chapter. However, for those who have the time to consider these issues then I encourage you to continue reading through the rest of this chapter. Your time will not be wasted!

Peter's developing theology

But what of Peter's developing theology resulting from his memories of Jesus and interpreted as his own life matured? How did his progressing life impact upon Mark's writing of the Gospel? The obvious place to look for this development is in the letters attributed to Peter. However, there is considerable scholarly disagreement as to whether or not the three letters in question are authentically Peter. From my research, I am happy to go with the arguments which indeed suggest that 1 Peter is an authentic pastoral letter written in 64 or 65 CE. However, it may well have been delegated to a Greek-speaking scribe, perhaps even Mark himself, to actually write. Notice the word 'delegate' rather than 'dictate'! This letter develops Peter's understanding of the place of suffering and persecution within the lives of those who follow the Jesus Way. To the persecuted Christian communities in northern Asia Minor Peter offered encouragement from his own experience of persecution in Rome.

His letter appealed to his scattered followers to remain faithful to their calling even though many of their number had already died for the faith, and persecution could fall upon any follower at any time. William J. Dalton, SJ summarizes the essentially 'keep the faith' doctrines contained in 1 Peter as follows:

> By emphasizing the dignity of the Christian vocation, which provides a God-given 'home' for the 'homeless', and the positive value of sharing the passion of Christ through persecution, the writer encourages his readers to remain faithful. These two themes run through the whole letter, but reach high points in the texts such as 2:4-10 ("the spiritual house") and 2:18-25 (directly dealing with slaves but valid

> for all Christians). The climax of the letter seems to come in 3:18-4:6, where Christians' confidence in persecution is seen as based on the story of Christ's salvific acts.

Even though being a follower of the Jesus Way can be uncomfortable or even deadly, this 'keep the faith' theme also runs throughout the Gospel of Mark. Amidst the rejections of Jesus and the various attempts to destroy him, Mark has the victory of suffering shining through. This obviously culminates in the suffering and death of Jesus, especially in the recognition of Jesus being the Son of God coming, not from a Jew but from a gentile Roman soldier [15:39]. Not even death was the end. In Peter's experience there was sanctity in suffering.

It may be a surprise to many readers but there is no merit in us exploring Peter's theology in the 2nd Letter attributed to him. Although many conservative New Testament scholars still hold to the tradition that 2 Peter is authentically from Peter the Apostle, the general scholarly understanding now is that 2 Peter was not written until at least the end of the first century. It contains much of the Letter of Jude which is dated usually between 90 and 100 CE. 2 Peter also makes references to the apostles as though they were people of the past rather than of the present.

The arguments in favor of discounting 2 Peter as being authentically Peter the Apostle have been made by scholars such as Burton L. Mack, Raymond E. Brown, Andrew Chester, and Jack Spong. Indeed, Spong explicitly links Jude 1:7 and 2 Peter 2:6 in his book *The Sins of Scripture* as those frequently used by Christians who shield themselves behind verses cherry-picked out of context as they seek to justify biblical negativity in support of their own homophobia. Spong [p. 141] points out that neither of these verses actually speaks at all about homosexuality but were intended to illustrate what was thought to be God's destructive power against those who did not believe [Jude] and to attack teachers of heresy [2 Peter].

I constantly remind people that there are several important starting points when considering the 'Christian' Gospels that were selected in 367 CE. by Athanasius:

- Not one of them was written as a Gospel. Each was a record of the experiences of distinct and particular communities as they remembered and interpreted the life and death of Jesus.

- They were not written for you or for me. They were literature written and used for teaching and encouragement within the communities of the authors.

- They were written at different times and within varying social contexts. When we read any of the Christian Testament today we need to keep in mind two time scales. The first relates to what Jesus really did and said which had occurred several decades before the writing of any texts. The second was when the Gospels and letters were written as interpretations of historical memories and as records of developing theology. These two time scale/contexts are also impacted upon by place and socio-political conditions within which the writing about the earlier events took place. To miss or to ignore these contextual time settings will lead to misinterpreting what the writers were trying to say.

The Gospels should be read in the order of their writing to see the social commentary reflecting the different and developing social, political and religious contexts of the later communities of Matthew and then Luke, followed by John, develop into an emerging theology of Jesus and God.

If this premise is correct then Mark is more social commentary than it is developed theology. Not only does it include the stories and memories of the Apostle Peter but it also contains Peter's development of elementary theology concerning Jesus of Nazareth. In this Peter thought of Jesus as being so full of humanity that he knew, in him, that he had met divinity.

Hierarchy and exploitation

The social commentary of Mark also demonstrated that the social organization of the day was one of hierarchy and exploitation. It had been that way even in the lifetime of Jesus – James and John wanted to be at the right and left hands of Jesus in glory! Even Paul and Peter may have been party to such hierarchy in the development of early Christianity with its overseers (bishops), elders (presbyters), and deacons (assistants) referenced in the letter to the Philippians [1:1]. This was probably written originally as three separate letters from the Apostle Paul living under house arrest in Rome between 54 and his execution. Such hierarchy crops up again in 1 Timothy.

But as Peter's theology developed, the social commentary of hierarchy was contrasted with what he remembered and subsequently interpreted to be the Jesus Way – it was that those who wished to be first will be last and the last will be first [Mark 9:34-36; Mark 10:30-32; Matthew 19:29-30; Matthew 20:15-17; Luke 13:29-31; Thomas 3]. Jesus lived and proclaimed servant-hood and even washed the feet of the disciples. According to the story, Jesus said that to be the greatest in the Kingdom, you have to be the least important – the *agape* servant of all.

> 43Not so with you. Instead, whoever wants to become great among you must be your servant, 44and whoever wants to be first must be slave of all. 45For even the Son of Man did not come to be served, but to serve, and to give his life as a ransom for many.
> [Mark 10:43-45 (New International Version); repeated in Matthew 20:25-28; alluded to in Thomas 11?]

Mark's social commentary also indicates that, at that time, it was the social norm for people to be considered as either 'for' or 'against' – as to being ' in' or 'out' of the different communities and social

gatherings. But Mark's Jesus said, "Anyone who is not against us is for us." No religious group could then, or even today, claim to have the only and the whole truth and nothing but the truth. Perhaps Jesus was simply saying that any Jew who was not against his teaching was to be counted for his teaching? Or, as Jesus continued his slow change from the narrow-minded exclusivism of his Judaism into the liberty of all who will may come, did Mark's Jesus mean Jew, gentile, male, female, Greek and even members of the Roman Empire?
Note, however, that Matthew's community suffered in different ways to that of Peter/Mark and experienced this Jesus saying as being the exact opposite:

> 30Whoever is not with me is against me, and whoever does not gather with me scatters. [Matthew 12:30 (New International Version)]

This is explored in greater detail in *Setting Jesus Free* [pages 75-81].

Holiness by separation
The Jewish belief, even upheld in the early ministry of Jesus, was that their holiness by separation [that's how the 613 commandments of the Law came to be interpreted] was what brought them as one people out of exile in Egypt and later from Babylon. It also helped them survive earlier military occupations by Persians, Greeks and Seleucids and it was believed that such separation would bring them out of Roman occupation. However, Jesus had developed beyond this holiness by separation when he began to accept gentiles as followers of his Way and this was one of the major reasons why the Pharisees, Sadducees and other Jewish sects turned against him. When his disciples later, especially post-70 CE, continued to accept gentiles into the synagogues, the whole basis of holiness by separation leading to eventual self-determined political, economic and religious freedom was being undermined.

Also, it should be noted that Judaism probably survived the

destruction of the Temple – the place of meeting between the High Priest and Yahweh in the Holy of Holies – because the Pharisees had already attempted to supplement the Temple Cult with a series of local synagogues as centers of worship and community.
Judaism had a number of smaller sects and the geographical dispersion of these enabled some of them to survive the final defeat at Masada in 73 CE.

It is my contention that the Christian Testament should be read and interpreted today within as much of the social context of the writing that we can discover. To read the Christian Testament at a superficial literalist level serves only to corrupt the original message and lifestyle of Jesus and also of the thinking and experiences of the Christian Testament writers in the 7 decades after the execution of Jesus.

So how much do we really know about Jesus of Nazareth? From the Markan evidence Jesus may still have been living in Nazareth at the time that he went to John the Baptist, somewhere along the Jordan River. After his baptism, Jesus is said to have spent 40 days in the wilderness, and then returned to the area alongside the Sea of Galilee where he began to call his early disciples. But was it 12 disciples from the start or was it a slow gathering of a ministerial team?

We now commence studying the Gospel of Mark chapter by chapter. Having a Bible to hand may be useful!

Mark Chapter 1:
Calling the first disciples (inconsistent Gospel accounts)

A third of the way through the first chapter of Mark's Gospel the fishermen Simon (Peter), Andrew, James and John, all probably from the fishing village of Bethsaida, no more than 5 miles to the northeast of Capernaum, accepted the invitation of Jesus to join him. They went together to Capernaum, an important strategic town built on the strip of land between the Capernaum Mountain and the Sea of Galilee.

But here again it is obvious that the other three Gospels adapted the Peter/Mark story and, as such, they were not writing accurate history of the calling of the earliest group of disciples. Mark 1:16-20 has Jesus simply walking along the shoreline at Capernaum. The fame of Jesus was spreading throughout the region so much so that Simon and his brother Andrew doubtless would have been aware of this travelling itinerant preacher. They must have been impressed by what they had seen and heard so that, when Jesus reached them beside their fishing boat and invited them to leave their fishing nets and to go with him to become fishers of men, they gave up everything, without question, to follow Jesus. A short while later they were passing James and John who were in a fishing boat with their father and, to the same invitation, the two brothers gave up everything to go with Jesus.

In Matthew 4:18-22 there is the same story, virtually word for word as in Mark's account, merely adding a little note that James and John did not leave their father completely in the lurch because their father still had hired hands to help him. However, in Luke there is much more detail, but again often contradictory to the earlier accounts in both Mark and Matthew. The Luke story of the calling of the earliest disciples starts with a prior incident. The Gospel of Thomas 32 is reflected in Luke 4:21-30 that tells of Jesus making that disastrous visit to his home synagogue in Nazareth. From there Jesus went to Capernaum and into that synagogue on the next Sabbath where he healed a man with an evil spirit.

From the synagogue Jesus went to the home of Simon who, as far as we can tell from this account, had not previously met Jesus [Luke 4:31-44]. When Jesus arrived at Simon's house he was told that Simon's mother-in-law was sick with a fever. But as soon as Jesus heard of the fever, he went to her and ordered the fever to leave. At once, according to Luke, she was able to get up and resumed her normal duties of cooking a meal for Jesus and the family.

The news went around fast so that, after the sun had set on that Sabbath day, people with all kinds of illnesses were brought to Jesus. As I read this Luke's account, I feel sorry for Simon. I think that it is implicit that, with the crowd still there, Simon had to leave the gathering to go to work on his fishing boat.

The next morning [Luke 5:1-11] Jesus departed from Simon's house and attempted to find a place to be alone. But the crowds went looking for him, seeking more healing and more wisdom. To escape the gathering crush of people, Jesus looked around him and saw two fishing boats with the fishermen cleaning their nets after their night's work. One of the fishermen was Simon. Jesus went to him, got into the boat and asked Simon to row a little offshore.

Can you imagine the reaction of Simon who, after an abortive night's fishing, just wanted to go home for some sleep but his new passenger, Jesus, asked him to push the boat out? (But isn't that what following Jesus always means, constantly pushing the boat out to do new things and to take risks for the Kingdom, even when we are tired and exhausted?) No matter what Simon thought he obeyed and rowed a little offshore to create some space between Jesus and the gathering crowd. From the safety of the boat Jesus could teach but he was not in a position to touch or to heal. And then, when Jesus had said enough he knew that it was time to stop talking and to leave. Doubtless the crowd wanted him to stay and to continue teaching, but popularity and personality are not adequate reasons to remain doing the same thing just because the people want to listen, to hear and to experience more.

Then, to make matters worse for poor Simon, Jesus asked him to row the boat out to deeper water and to let his nets down again in an attempt to catch some fish. This was after Simon and the crew of his boat had already done a night's fishing without any success. Can you imagine Simon's response of miserable submission? In my imagination Simon is under some stress, perhaps thinking, "What do you know about fishing? I am the fisherman. I know when the fish are not there. I am tired and I want to go home."

One of my favorite descriptions of stress is "When the head says 'no' but the mouth says, 'I would love to'!" I have been there and I have worn the sweatshirt! But then Simon speaks, "We have worked hard all night long and caught nothing (that's the head talking) but if you tell me, then I will let the nets down" (that's the mouth talking!).

Luke demonstrated, not for the last time, that obeying Jesus and taking Kingdom risks paid dividends. So many fish were caught that the nets began to break. Simon called for the other boat to come and help. The catch was so great that both boats were in danger of sinking. (The message may be that taking a Kingdom risk is often dangerous but the rewards are often greater?)

As I read the Luke version I wonder who was crewing the boat that came to the rescue. Luke 5:10 suggests that it was James and John, the sons of Zebedee, partners with Simon. They were amazed at the size of the catch. The impact was such that Simon realized that he was in the presence of someone much greater than himself.

This became for Simon a truly sacred experience. It is the awe and wonder of such a catch represented by the extraordinary within the ordinary things of life that have become a spiritual experience for him. It can be so for us, suddenly seeing the extraordinary within the ordinary. For example, my breath was taken away when I first looked down into it and across the grandeur of the Grand Canyon. All its amazing colors just made me go, "'Wow." It happened for me in Boulder where, in the space of 24 hours in mid-May 2010, I experienced all four seasons of the year. I still have similar breathtaking moments when travelling around the English

Lake District and suddenly coming upon another magnificent lake, especially in the warm summer glows of a brilliant fiery sunset. It also happened when I first touched my newly born daughter's small delicate fingers way back in 1975 and again those of my son in 1978 – both of these moments were and remain spiritual experiences for me. But too often I spend too much of my time looking for the extraordinary beyond the ordinary – or perhaps I don't look at all? Either way, I miss the blessing of being aware of God in all things and all things in God.

As the nets began to break, Simon fell to his knees before Jesus and the response of Jesus was life changing: "There is no need to be afraid. From here on in you will be fishers of men."

Luke's account of the calling of these earliest disciples concludes with the clear statement that they left everything and went with Jesus.

However, when we look for this story of the calling of the first disciples in the Gospel of John we will look in vain because it simply is not there. Instead, it is a story subsequently used by the author of John's Gospel as the post-resurrection BBQ on the seashore [John 21:1-12].

There are further contradictions to the other Gospel stories concerning the calling of the first disciples. John's account already has Andrew, Simon's brother, a disciple of John the Baptist. Then, when Andrew and an unnamed friend met Jesus for the first time, Andrew and his companion left the Baptist and immediately went with Jesus.

So impressed was Andrew that he went to Simon and said, "We have found the Messiah." Simon went with Andrew to meet Jesus, and Jesus adds 'Peter' (the rock) to Simon's name. We do not know from this account whether or not Andrew's companion continued with Jesus or returned to John the Baptist. But this passage continues [John 1:43-51] on the next day with Andrew, Simon Peter and Jesus going back into Galilee, through Andrew and Simon Peter's hometown of either Bethsaida or close-by Capernaum. It is there that they met with Philip, who also gave up everything to follow Jesus.

Philip then told Nathanael and he also joined this small but growing band of disciples. Then three days later, and some 25 miles west of Bethsaida, Jesus and his four named disciples were with his mother, brothers and sisters at a wedding feast in Cana [John 2:1-12]. So much for the additions and contradictions to the Peter / Mark original account of these callings – surely not all four inconsistent accounts can be correct and accurate history?

Jesus goes to Capernaum

As we return to Mark's Gospel it is important to note that it begins, not with Jesus of Nazareth, but with John the Baptist. Then in Mark 1:12-13 Jesus, following his baptism, went into the desert for 40 days. I will not explore this episode as I have written more about this time in the desert in *Setting Jesus Free* [pages 36-38] where I delve into the possibility that Jesus was in the process of becoming a 'nazir', set aside for God's purposes.

But Mark 1:14-15 always holds a surprise for me. After John the Baptist's arrest, Jesus of Nazareth arrived on the public scene somewhere in Galilee. As the eldest son, surely it was the place of Jesus, after his baptism and sojourn in the wilderness, to be back in Nazareth with the family business? So why did Jesus lead his small band of new disciples to nearby Capernaum rather than to his hometown of Nazareth?

Capernaum was a town some 20 miles to the northeast near the Sea of Galilee, on the road from the Galilee region to Damascus. Perhaps it was because he and his family fell out over some argument or other associated with the business? Or perhaps Jesus was becoming too interested in the spiritual that they considered him to be of no earthly use?

I also wonder if this was one of the reasons why, at a later date, Jesus was so devastatingly rejected by his family and neighbors in his original hometown of Nazareth? Did they despise him because, in their opinion, they should have been basking in the glow of his growing reputation, but instead it was Capernaum where the glow settled?

There is another possibility in that Jesus really did exercise his familial responsibilities by taking his widowed mother and younger brothers and sisters with him as they settled into his new home in Capernaum. But whether or not Jesus has his family with him modern translations are more or less in agreement that Jesus was 'at home' in Capernaum. "When Jesus returned to Capernaum several days later, the news spread quickly that he was back home." [Mark 2:1 (New International Version)]

Of course it could simply mean that Jesus felt very much at home, accepting the occasional hospitality of a well-wisher or follower of his way, perhaps even Simon Peter's mother-in-law? On the other hand, it could indicate that Jesus had actually set up a regular home in Capernaum, perhaps because it was such a strategic place on the road from Galilee to Damascus?

I am inclined to think that it was the latter. Jesus went to Capernaum to be involved in its synagogue and the way of life associated with it. As a result of the enthusiastic reception that he was given, the strategic significance of the town on the north-south road and the importance of the synagogue, Jesus decided that Capernaum was to be the headquarters of his mission to unite and to reform Judaism.

It was in researching material for this book that I came across archaeological evidence supporting my reasons for Capernaum becoming the base of the mission. Edward Robinson who, while undertaking extensive archaeological excavations in 1838, discovered the remains of the once prosperous town of Capernaum. It had been deserted and 'lost' since the 11th century. The Franciscans then acquired the site at the end of the 19th century and excavations continued through the 20th century. The excavations of Robinson, and of others since that time, have revealed that the synagogue that would have been visited by Jesus was a magnificent building constructed from local white limestone blocks. It was given prominence by having been built on a platform that towered over the surrounding houses and other basalt and cement buildings.

The houses of the wealthy (and there were many in the town) were built around courtyards, each with only one entrance onto the adjacent street. External staircases were built alongside the walls of the courtyard giving access to the second floor or to the roof. But unlike the other buildings in Capernaum, the synagogue had streets around all its four walls.

Perhaps it was owing to the splendor and importance of the synagogue that gave him a good base from which to develop his itinerant ministry intent on the unification and reformation of Judaism?

As mentioned a short while ago, having arrived in Capernaum Jesus and his four disciples attended the synagogue on the following Sabbath [Mark 1:21-29]. Here he amazed people by teaching with authority and by the casting out of an evil spirit.

Jesus started preaching that God's Kingdom would soon be present, so they should turn back to God and believe the good news! An obvious implication of this invitation to turn back to God was that, in the eyes of Jesus, some Capernaum Jews, under the leadership of the Pharisees, had been led astray from his developing understanding of God. This created some early antagonism among the self-righteous. Later this was allowed to fester into character assassination paving the way for an execution on a cross.

There is an explicit indication that the vision of Jesus was very different to the vision of the religious leadership of the Pharisees and the Sadducees, and the other sects of Judaism at that time. But reading the first chapter of Mark's Gospel gives no indication that Jesus was intentionally setting himself up against the Pharisees and Sadducees. Certainly he was not setting up an alternative Christian Church. There could have been nothing further from the mind of Jesus other than to unite, reform and rejuvenate Judaism. In fact, after many exorcisms and then that first healing of a leper, Jesus upheld the requirements of the Law of Moses by telling the healed leper that he should tell no one but to go straight to the priest and offer the sacrifices that Moses had commanded in response to cleansing and healing [Mark 1:40-45].

It was during that teaching and healing time in the Capernaum synagogue [Mark 1:24-28] that a man with an evil spirit entered the place and shouted at Jesus, demanding to know what Jesus wanted with him and the evil spirit. Although he recognized him as Jesus of Nazareth, he also added that both he and the evil spirit acknowledged him as the Holy One of God. They asked if Jesus had come to destroy them.

According to the Mark story, Jesus commanded the evil spirit to be quiet and to depart from the man. The man shook violently and screamed and the people interpreted this as the evil spirit departing from him. In amazement the people asked one another if this was a new teaching, especially because they witnessed an unusual authority that not only gave orders to evil spirits but that those spirits obeyed him.

In no time at all, news of this incident spread throughout Galilee. Remembering that no work was to be done on the Sabbath, Jesus had clearly broken the Law on this first Sabbath occasion in the Capernaum synagogue. Jesus had set down his marker – one that would make him a prophet to some and a heretic to others.

Although I have previously referenced the Luke account, Mark also has Jesus, still on the Sabbath, going immediately from the synagogue and healing Simon's mother-in-law. The opposition from the Sadducees and Pharisees was bound to grow, but as far as many of the ordinary people were concerned Jesus had done nothing wrong. Indeed, that very evening after the sun had set many who were ill and / or demon-possessed were brought to Jesus [Mark 1:32]. Note that 'after sunset' was also after the end of the Sabbath.

Also note that at that time, according to Mark's Gospel, there was no accusation or condemnation of the action of Jesus on the part of the Pharisees and Sadducees – probably because the news of the

Sabbath exorcism had not yet reached them. But the writing was on the wall if not in the Gospel text – for Jesus to heal on the Sabbath was breaking the Law.

But just as troublesome and threatening was that Jesus had been publicly recognized as having more Godly authority than the official spiritual leadership of Pharisees and Sadducees. This was setting Jesus on a collision course with the religious and political Jewish elite. I even think that there was something naive about Jesus and his early ministry, thinking that he could take on the religious establishment and reform it. Although a head of steam sometimes gathers around a hugely popular cause resulting in successful reformation, it seems to me that, more often than not, the power of the Establishment eventually destroys the reformer.

The theology of the early disciples

It is necessary for us to recognize that there is a world of difference between what we think we know about Jesus, possibly because the Church and its preachers have told us the story in certain ways, and who the historical Jesus really was. Only in the past two centuries has the quest for the historical Jesus and for an authentic Jesus message given rise to an increasing number of new insights that radically challenge the creedal versions and interpretations of the Church concerning Jesus of Nazareth.

In these very early days in the ministry of Jesus the theology of the disciples and ordinary followers alike seems to have not yet developed beyond "Jesus of Nazareth – the Holy One sent from God" into "Jesus, Son of God". The most that Peter and Mark had the demoniac declare was [24] "What do you want with us, Jesus of Nazareth? Have you come to destroy us? I know who you are—the Holy One of God!" [Mark 1:24 (New International Version)] Notice that Jesus was not recognized at that time as the Son of God, only one who had been sent by God. But even in being sent by God, his actions created problems for some because Jesus had healed on the Sabbath.

The transformation from 'sent from God' to 'Son of God' began to happen, at least for Peter, only after Jesus had declared himself to be 'Son of Man' [Mark 2:28]. Whereas people had yet to see Jesus as Son of God, Peter's memory of the incident between Jesus and evil spirits was that the spirit world already recognized that status [Mark 2:12].

The morning after those Sabbath day healings Jesus withdrew for his customary time of solitude so that he could pray. The outcome was a decision that he and his disciples needed to leave the area and to travel to the synagogues and meeting places throughout Galilee. Jesus then took his four disciples (note: at this stage, still only four disciples!) and they started their first journey to the synagogues throughout Galilee, preaching and exorcising demons. That could have taken several weeks.

During these travels a leper approached Jesus [Mark 1:40-45]. The usual pattern was for those suffering from leprosy to be excluded from home and community. Certainly no one would actually touch a leper for fear of being 'infected' by leprosy. But once again, Jesus demonstrated that no one was beyond compassion. Jesus touched the man and healed him. The leper was told to tell no one but to go to the priest and fulfill the requirements of the Law of Moses.

So what, I wonder, are the implications of this story of the leper for life today? Perhaps it is that we who are the 'respectable' and the 'religious' need to treat no one as inferior or unclean? Perhaps we need to be much more open to and accepting of difference? And that includes especially those who are the excluded and the social outcasts?

Notice, however, that even Jesus was at the mercy of the actions and reactions of others. The leper was so overjoyed at his miraculous healing that he went and told everybody whom he met. The result was that Jesus had to abandon his planned ministry to the towns and he fled to the wilderness areas. Yet, even there, people flocked out to see, to hear and, in many cases, to be healed.

Mark Chapter 2:
Jesus sets up his home in Capernaum

According to the narrative as detailed at the beginning of Mark Chapter 2, Jesus and his four disciples returned to Capernaum.

It was now, early in the ministry of Jesus, that what he was doing and saying brought him to the attention of the Pharisees. It was here in Capernaum that Mark's Gospel first mentions that some of the Pharisees were sitting, watching and wondering about Jesus. The incident took place in the home of Jesus. The room was packed out with people listening to the teaching and watching the healing ministry of Jesus. Then four people arrived carrying a crippled man on a mat. The men could not get into the house of Jesus so they climbed the external stairs onto the roof, broke open the beams and boards covered in packed earth and let the man down into the center of things.

I know that the architecture of homes then was very different to that of my home, and the roof covering may well have been designed for removal in hot weather. However, the reaction of Jesus was far from what mine would have been had someone come along and, without invitation, made a hole in my roof! Jesus did not get angry or become impolite. He simply looked at the faith of the friends of the man and said, "Your sins are forgiven. Your faith has healed you."

This is a significant comment: it was the faith of the friends and not any direct supernatural intervention 'from above' that healed the man. So often in the healing ministry of Jesus the comment was time and again, "Your faith has healed you." There is no doubt in my mind that miraculous healings took place then and take place today. In my experience as a one-time evangelical charismatic church leader, I know that the more charismatic churches both experience and interpret such healings as supernatural blessings from God.

Long-standing friends who travelled with me down the evangelical charismatic years remain in that branch of the Church and for some years now have been ministering in South Africa. I quote, with permission, from their Christmas letter for 2009:

> We regularly see God's touch on peoples' lives who testify to healing. As well as headaches, joint pains, back problems, and relief from other common ailments, we have also witnessed several miraculous healings from cancer and AIDS related diseases. One guy went back to the hospital to be rescanned 4 times to try and find the tumors he had been diagnosed with, only to be pronounced as completely healed. Another lady was in 'end stage' AIDS, rapidly losing weight, unable to walk and confined to bed in a local hospice a year ago. Mary spent many days taking her to an amazing doctor at the public hospital, who would not give up on her; but even he had to admit in February that he could do nothing more for her and advised us to prepare her for the inevitable! We had been praying with her all along, but we now decided to find a way to bring her to the healing room where we encourage people to 'soak' in the presence of God and then anoint them with oil before praying for them. From that moment we have seen a miraculous recovery and she is now discharged from the hospice and looking to study further and even apply for a job! Everyone who knows her says that she is a walking miracle and an amazing testimony that God is our healer and deliverer.

However, I now look beyond the surface of such healings and see them much more as the result of the incredible capacity of the human spirit, enabled, encouraged and empowered by the indwelling sacred Namaste Spirit. This combination of individual spirit and Namaste Spirit invigorates the expectation of healing. When supported and encouraged by the Namaste love, prayers and symbolic actions of those who are concerned with the person who is suffering, then spontaneous healing can more easily take place. Tillich also expressed something similar when he wrote that everyone has both the potential and the priestly responsibility to heal anyone. He also said that this healing power is available whether or not people are church members or ministers (1963, p. 59).

So is the South Africa example of healing miraculous? Yes it is. But is it a revelation of a Supreme Interventionist God? Not in my understanding because, in my experience, 'God' is a three letter descriptor of the indescribable presence of the sacred both within and beyond each one of us. 'God' is shorthand for describing the sacred experience, but such description is always limited by human language. However, such miracles are signs of the sacred that is available to all because the Sacred Namaste Spirit indwells all people.

Also, in the context of the first recorded healing at the hands of Jesus in his own home, note that Jesus did not first say, "You are healed – get up and walk!" Jesus saw the faith of the four friends and turned to the disabled man and said, "Son, your sins are forgiven." The Pharisees began muttering to one another, "Why does this fellow talk like that? He's blaspheming! Who can forgive sins but God alone?"

I am not convinced that Jesus recognized the magnitude of what he was taking on, but Mark's literary construction is already signposting the battle that is to shortly unfold.

After the disabled man had been healed, Jesus went through the town to the shore of Lake Galilee. There he saw Levi Matthew, a hated collaborator with Rome, a reviled tax collector treated by both Pharisees and ordinary people as a traitor. He along with many Jewish tax collectors exploited their own people to line their own pockets. Levi Matthew brought dishonor upon the Jewish people. However, whereas the Pharisees rejected Levi Matthew, Jesus saw in him a fellow human being who was worth more than all his ill-gotten finances.

Jesus invited Levi to follow him, and he did just that! [Mark 2:14] This is how I understand conversion. It is not simply about a prayer of repentance and all will be well for eternity. It is a complete about-face in the way that a person thinks and acts. It is about a conscious transformation of self into the image of Jesus. Levi Matthew not only invited Jesus and his four disciples for a meal, but he also invited other reviled tax collectors to come and experience something of the life and compassion of Jesus.

While this Capernaum meal was underway, some Pharisees came and were appalled by what they saw. They asked his disciples why Jesus ate with those who they (the Pharisees) considered to be tax collectors and 'sinners' [Mark 2:16]. Jesus overheard the question and not only responded with a pointed comment but also, as part of Mark's literary device, laid down the direction of his ministry: "It is not the healthy who need a doctor, but the sick. I have not come to call the righteous, but sinners." [Mark 2: 17 (New International Version)]

Jesus and a united and reformed Judaism

In the thinking of Jesus, a united and reformed Judaism would not be concerned with the Pharisaic slavish maintaining of the Law of Moses to decide who was 'in' and who was 'out'. Notice three important points at this stage in the ministry of Jesus:

- A united and reformed Judaism would no longer differentiate between Jews of the several different Jewish sects of the time.

- Yahweh God was still God of the Jews alone, and not interested in the welfare of gentiles. That would have to wait a little longer before the mind of Jesus expanded so that Yahweh was seen as God of all people, Jew and gentile alike.

- Nor would a united and reformed Judaism commit its followers to religious fasting. Some ordinary people were as perplexed as the Pharisees by Jesus eating with the tax collectors. This was compounded by the fact that a religious fast was underway at the time. The disciples of John the Baptist and those who closely followed the example and teaching of the Pharisees were abstaining from food on religious grounds. Mark has Jesus responding to their questions:

> [19]Jesus answered, "How can the guests of the bridegroom fast while he is with them? They cannot, so long as they have him with them. [20]But the time will come when the bridegroom will be taken from them, and on that day they will fast. [21]"No one sews a patch of unshrunk cloth on an old garment. Otherwise, the new piece will pull away from the old, making the tear worse. [22]And no one pours new wine into old wineskins. Otherwise, the wine will burst the skins, and both the wine and the wineskins will be ruined. No, they pour new wine into new wineskins." [Mark 2:19-22 (New International Version)]

In the memory and interpretation of Peter, the message was clear: Jesus set out as a religious reformer based within prophetic Judaism. However, in retrospect Peter concluded that the uniting and reforming work of Jesus could not and did not remain at just tinkering at the edge. As the ministry of reformation gathered pace it threatened to become a root and branch transformation based upon compassion rather than legalism. It also developed in the thinking and actions of Jesus so that the exclusivism of Judaism, in that Yahweh was God of the Jews alone, gave way to understanding Yahweh as God of Jew and gentile alike. It was as Peter looked back over the intervening 20 years, he realized that what he had experienced with Jesus was that legalistic Judaism could not be reformed: it was the old cloth that could not cope with the new cloth of Jesus; it was the old wine skin that could not accommodate the new wine of Jesus.

I wonder what this says about the institutional church attempts in Britain to develop 'new ways of being church'; of 'Fresh Expressions' when it is just the same old package of creeds and doctrines wrapped up in new zip zap clothing? What is needed is not new packaging but a new product – or rather, the authentic product of the pre-Easter

Jesus of Nazareth!

After the execution of Jesus, Peter almost walked away even before the vision began to take place in his experience. He actually returned to what he was used to, no longer a fisher of men but back to fishing in Lake Galilee. However, the ongoing presence of the Namaste Jesus Spirit in his life would not give him rest. The Jesus Spirit convinced him that he, too, should return to the work of reformation that Jesus had let go while dying on the cross.

Although Peter got so many things wrong in his time with Jesus, and even later in his managerial and theological conflicts with Paul, James, John and Mary Magdalene, he had learned that Yahweh's love was not just for Jews but for all people. That is what the story of Pentecost is all about: "Fellow Jews and all of you who live in Jerusalem, let me explain this to you; listen carefully to what I say." [Acts 2:14] Notice that the message of what Yahweh God had done and what Yahweh was doing was for Jew and gentile alike. And yet, even at Pentecost Peter had not learned an important message concerning the grace of his Yahweh God: that gentiles did not first have to become Jews to become followers of Jesus. I suggest that that realization had to wait until the Joppa vision and Cornelius.

> [9]About noon the following day as they were on their journey and approaching the city, Peter went up on the roof to pray. [10]He became hungry and wanted something to eat, and while the meal was being prepared, he fell into a trance. [11]He saw heaven opened and something like a large sheet being let down to earth by its four corners. [12]It contained all kinds of four-footed animals, as well as reptiles and birds. [13]Then a voice told him, "Get up, Peter. Kill and eat."
>
> [14]"Surely not, Lord!" Peter replied. "I have never eaten anything impure or unclean."
>
> [15]The voice spoke to him a second time, "Do not call anything impure that God has made clean." [Acts 10:9-15 (New International Version)]

Later still Paul the Apostle to the gentiles, the fulfilled Jew Saul of Tarsus, also argued that it was not necessary for gentiles to become Jews before they could be Christians. His message was that Yahweh equally loved Jew and gentile, just as they were, and without any discrimination or need for gentiles to become Jews before they could become Christians. All people were Temples inhabited by God's Spirit and therefore they were already fit and proper before Yahweh God.

In the days of Abiathar – did God sanction rape?

According to the narrative we continue in Capernaum. In the early days of the ministry of Jesus of Nazareth we find him with his disciples walking through a wheat field on a Sabbath. According to Mark there were some Pharisees watching and waiting to see if Jesus broke any more Sabbath Laws. They saw what they wanted to see – the disciples were hungry and they plucked the grain and ate it. The Pharisees complained but Jesus had an answer and an explanation for them.

> [25]He answered, "Have you never read what David did when he and his companions were hungry and in need? [26] In the days of Abiathar the high priest, he entered the house of God and ate the consecrated bread, which is lawful only for priests to eat. And he also gave some to his companions." [Mark 2:25-26 (New International Version)]

I wonder how many Christians, preachers included, have just taken this answer at face value. But it raises a number of questions for me starting with something for those who approach the Bible with the understanding that it can be read as literal truth, free of all error: "How can the Bible be without error when Mark records Jesus having specifically said that it was from Abiathar that David took the bread of the Presence when, in fact, it was taken from Ahimelech the priest?" The story is in 1 Samuel 21:1-6.

[1]David went to Nob, to Ahimelek the priest.
Ahimelek trembled when he met him, and asked,
"Why are you alone? Why is no one with you?"
[2]David answered Ahimelek the priest, "The king
sent me on a mission and said to me, 'No one is to
know anything about the mission I am sending you
on.' As for my men, I have told them to meet me at
a certain place. [3] Now then, what do you have on
hand? Give me five loaves of bread, or whatever
you can find."
[4]But the priest answered David, "I don't have any
ordinary bread on hand; however, there is some
consecrated bread here – provided the men have
kept themselves from women."
[5]David replied, "Indeed women have been kept
from us, as usual whenever I set out. The men's
bodies are holy even on missions that are not holy.
How much more so today!" [6]So the priest gave him
the consecrated bread, since there was no bread
there except the bread of the Presence that had been
removed from before the LORD and replaced by
hot bread on the day it was taken away.
(New International Version)

Within this passage I find another Hebrew Testament situation that is totally incompatible with my understanding of the sacred that I meet in Jesus. It concerns the conduct of military personnel towards women while they were on their warring travels. It is most unlikely that warriors then were accompanied into battle by their spouses. Therefore such a reference to Ahimelech the priest's question about the men keeping themselves from women must indicate that it was a norm to have the warriors of Yahweh God 'taking' women along the way. But who were these women? Perhaps they were prostitutes, in which case it was exploitation of those who had little with which to preserve their life other than their own bodies. Or were they part of the plunder and spoils of war, women who were not on the side of Yahweh God's warriors raped by the victorious soldiers?

> [10]When you march up to attack a city, make its people an offer of peace. [11]If they accept and open their gates, all the people in it shall be subject to forced labor and shall work for you. [12]If they refuse to make peace and they engage you in battle, lay siege to that city. [13]When the LORD your God delivers it into your hand, put to the sword all the men in it. [14]As for the women, the children, the livestock and everything else in the city, you may take these as plunder for yourselves. And you may use the plunder the LORD your God gives you from your enemies. [15]This is how you are to treat all the cities that are at a distance from you and do not belong to the nations nearby. [Deuteronomy 20:10-15 (New International Version)]

But there is further even more worrying 'legalized' rape of powerless women taken captive in combat.

> [10]When you go to war against your enemies and the LORD your God delivers them into your hands and you take captives, [11]if you notice among the captives a beautiful woman and are attracted to her, you may take her as your wife. [12]Bring her into your home and have her shave her head, trim her nails [13]and put aside the clothes she was wearing when captured. After she has lived in your house and mourned her father and mother for a full month, then you may go to her and be her husband and she shall be your wife. [14]If you are not pleased with her, let her go wherever she wishes. You must not sell her or treat her as a slave, since you have dishonored her. [Deuteronomy 21:10-14 (New International Version)]

The ritual of head shaving and so on was a process of conversion so that the Jewish warrior was no longer marrying a foreigner but she would be a convert to Judaism. Forced conversion and its accompanying 'legalized' rape, then and now, was and remains evil. Undoubtedly this passage fits into the 'warrior God' image of early Judaism. This is an image that I cannot reconcile with my understanding and experience of the sacred. Surely, no 'God' would ever condone or at the least turn a blind eye to such outrageous offences against women who are on the losing side in a battle?

Also, when thinking about this passage in Mark 2, I have to ask how was it possible that Jesus mixed up Abiathar and Ahimelech? Perhaps they were the same person but a later scribe corrupted the name? But that is not an acceptable answer as 1 Samuel 22:20 clearly states that Abiathar was a son of Ahimelech! This suggests then that either Jesus was mistaken or Peter mixed up the father and the son in the story of David taking the consecrated bread of the Presence, something that only priests were entitled to consume? Or the Gospels of Matthew and Luke may hold the answer in that both tell this story but neither includes references to Abiathar or Ahimelech.

> 1At that time Jesus went through the grainfields on the Sabbath. His disciples were hungry and began to pick some heads of grain and eat them. 2When the Pharisees saw this, they said to him, "Look! Your disciples are doing what is unlawful on the Sabbath."
>
> 3He answered, "Haven't you read what David did when he and his companions were hungry? 4He entered the house of God, and he and his companions ate the consecrated bread – which was not lawful for them to do, but only for the priests. 5Or haven't you read in the Law that the priests on Sabbath duty in the temple desecrate the Sabbath and yet are innocent? 6I tell you that something greater than the temple is here. 7If you had known what these words mean, 'I desire mercy, not sacrifice,' you would not have condemned the innocent. 8For

the Son of Man is Lord of the Sabbath."
[Matthew 12:1-8 (New International Version)]

The similar passage from Luke possibly indicates that the writers of both Gospels, Luke and Matthew, realized that Mark had made a mistake and corrected it by omitting any reference to the name of the priest involved?

[1]One Sabbath Jesus was going through the grainfields, and
his disciples began to pick some heads of grain, rub them in
their hands and eat the kernels. [2]Some of the Pharisees asked,
"Why are you doing what is unlawful on the Sabbath?"
[3]Jesus answered them, "Have you never read what David did
when he and his companions were hungry? [4]He entered the
house of God, and taking the consecrated bread, he ate what
is lawful only for priests to eat. And he also gave some to his
companions." [5]Then Jesus said to them, "The Son of Man is
Lord of the Sabbath."
[Luke 6:1-5 (New International Version)]

So much for the inerrancy of Scripture! It seems obvious to me that Peter/Mark simply got it wrong.

"Jesus has to be killed."

Be that as it may, this passage is part of Mark's ongoing literary device to demonstrate to the readers and listeners that the rules and regulations of the religion along with the Law of Moses rigidly applied was not what Kingdom living was really concerned with. Is this a message for us today as some churches are split by attitudes of antagonism towards and rejection of, for example, gays and lesbians?

Mark has stories from Chapter 1 through to Chapter 3 where work on the Sabbath brought confrontations with the Pharisees. In Mark's mind this was setting the direction of the ministry of Jesus as he told stories of confrontation:

• In Mark 2:1-12 there is confrontation when Jesus, in his own house, heals the disabled man and forgives his sins.

• In Mark 2:18-22 there is the confrontation sparked by Jesus and his disciples not fasting when the 'religious' people were doing so.

• In Mark 2:23-28 there is the confrontation because Jesus and the disciples took and ate the grain.

Mark has barely written 12% of the Gospel before the Pharisaic intent is clear, "Jesus has to be killed." The scene is now set and the rest of the Gospel will unfold with events that will inevitably end in an execution.

At the conclusion of the confrontation between Jesus and the Pharisees in that grain field, Jesus said to them that the Sabbath had been created for man, not the other way round. Therefore, according to the story, Jesus said that the Son of Man was Lord of the Sabbath as well! [Mark 2:27-28] Probably Jesus did say such as this but even if he had not, there must have been an immense impact upon the early Christian communities who were worshipping side by side in the synagogues with Jews who rejected the witness of Jesus. While these latter Jews continued to uphold the Sabbath Laws, this incident in which Peter/Mark have Jesus declaring himself to be Lord even of the Sabbath seems to me like an early Christian justification as to why the Jews and gentiles who followed the Jesus Way 30 years after his death treated the Sabbath so lightly.

Mark Chapter 3:

The decision to kill Jesus

Mark 3:1-6 continues straight on from the previous chapter with the Pharisees (the religious community leaders) and the Herodians (the political supporters of King Herod) conspiring together to rid themselves of Jesus. In this passage we read of another confrontation because Jesus has again healed on the Sabbath. This time it is a man with a withered hand. But Mark draws the series of confrontations to a close with something even more significant: "Then the Pharisees went out and began to plot with the Herodians how they might kill Jesus."

As a result of his wisdom teaching and healings the crowds begin to grow and doubtless many among them became regular followers wherever Jesus went. It is significant that Mark has evil spirits falling before Jesus and proclaiming that he is the Son of God. Once again I look upon this declaration as a hindsight theological addition [Mark 3:7-12].

Calling more disciples

Mark now says that Jesus selected others to become new members of his closest group of supporters. According to Peter/Mark, on a particular day Jesus invited a number of the wider group of followers to accompany him up the mountain. This was in all probability the highest point in the ridge of hills behind his adopted town, the Mount Capernaum.

> 14He appointed twelve that they might be with him and that he might send them out to preach 15and to have authority to drive out demons. 16These are the twelve he appointed: Simon (to whom he gave the name Peter), 17James son of Zebedee and his brother John (to them he gave the name Boanerges, which means 'sons of thunder'), 18 Andrew, Philip, Bartholomew, Matthew, Thomas, James son of Alphaeus, Thaddaeus, Simon the Zealot.

[Mark 3:14-18 (New International Version)]

Here is another Midrash in which Peter/Mark took the twelve tribes of Israel from the Hebrew Testament and assigned them to the reforming organization of Jesus' twelve apostles. In passing it should be noted that Matthew has the same list of disciples but Luke substitutes Thaddaeus with Judas, son of James. I am happy to be proved wrong but when I read John's Gospel I read that Jesus had twelve disciples but the only names that I can find are: Andrew, Simon Peter, Philip, Nathanael, Judas Iscariot, Thomas (called Didymus), and Judas (not Iscariot). There is one other reference to 'the disciple whom Jesus loved' (presumably John?). That I count as seven named plus one. I wonder why John left out the other four?

It should also be noted that there were dozens of disciples who followed his teaching [e.g. John 6:60-66]. However, it was the Peter/Mark recording of the appointment of apostles that was a further development of what was becoming the reformation work of Jesus. In the book *The Historical Jesus: Five Views* (2009) Crossan offers a telling comparison between John the Baptist and Jesus of Nazareth when he states that the ministry of John was a monopoly whereas Jesus developed a franchised ministry. As a consequence, when John was executed both his work and his disciples more or less disappeared.

Crossan further suggests that Jesus had learned from John's mistake. Rather than keep himself as the only central character, Jesus selected these twelve to train them to go and do the work that he himself was doing. In this way, should Jesus be executed as John had been, the work would not perish with his death. In today's management speak this would probably classify as training the trainers or equipping the sales force!

There comes now a further confrontation with the teachers of the Law who had travelled from Jerusalem. They accused Jesus of being possessed by Beelzebub, the prince of demons, to cast out demons. Jesus replied that such an accusation was nonsense as no house divided could survive [Mark 3:20-30]. One further interesting point from this passage is that the family of Jesus had become so concerned about his mental state they made up their minds to go and 'rescue' him from all that he was doing. Perhaps they could see the writing on the wall concerning the inevitability of the road that he was now travelling?

Now, as Mark's Gospel unfolds we reach a point of confusion as to geographic location of the story.

> Then Jesus entered a house, and again a crowd gathered, so that he and his disciples were not even able to eat. When his family heard about this, they went to take charge of him, for they said, "He is out of his mind." [Mark 3:20-21(New International Version)]

> And He came home, and the crowd gathered again, to such an extent that they could not even eat a meal. When His own people heard of this, they went out to take custody of Him; for they were saying, "He has lost His senses." [Mark 3:20-21 New American Standard Bible]

The English Standard Version is virtually identical although it says that Jesus went home, but was that his own home or a home? The Amplified Bible actually names the home as that probably belonging to Peter. It also talks about kinsmen rather than family but otherwise it has the same textual meaning.

So, if Jesus had not moved his family to Capernaum did he go back to his original home in Nazareth or were his mother, brothers and sisters so concerned about his mental well-being that they travelled some 20 miles to Capernaum to take charge of him intent on taking him back to their safekeeping in Nazareth? The Amplified Bible suggests that the house belonged to Peter and therefore it was in Capernaum. If it was his own home from where Jesus developed his ministry, then once more, according to the narrative, it had to be

Capernaum.
This is not a splitting of hairs but it is something that I consider to be most important in trying to understand Jesus, his family, his followers and what he was doing.

> [31]Then Jesus' mother and brothers arrived. Standing outside, they sent someone in to call him. [32]A crowd was sitting around him, and they told him, "Your mother and brothers are outside looking for you."
> [33]"Who are my mother and my brothers?" he asked.
> [34]Then he looked at those seated in a circle around him and said, "Here are my mother and my brothers! [35]Whoever does God's will is my brother and sister and mother."
> [Mark 3:31-35 (New International Version)]

The implication of this story of the encounter between Jesus and his family is that his mother, brothers and sisters all were failing to grasp his message and to realize the enormity of his transformational mission. Indeed, they were not doing God's will as far as Jesus saw it. All who were doing God's will concerning his mission to unite and to reform Judaism were now his adoptive family, his mother, brothers and sisters.

Although we are all indwelt by the same Namaste Spirit not all are 'doers' of God's will. We may be religious and keep all the commands. We may attend church regularly and recite the creeds, but unless we do the will of God then we are failing in our calling to be more human and consequently more divine. But the huge question is this: "What is the will of God?"

Mark Chapter 4:
Explaining the nature of the New Kingdom of God

This chapter considers some of the parables attributed to Jesus. After the encounter with his family, Jesus had to take to a boat because the crowds were so great. The boat was pushed just offshore and Jesus sat in it and began to teach again. He used stories that related with the experiences of the listeners [Mark 4:1-12]; but even so, Jesus explained a short while later to his disciples that: "They may be ever seeing but never perceiving, and ever hearing but never understanding; otherwise they might turn and be forgiven!" [Mark 4:12 (New International Version)]

I find that strange: to tell a story so that people can understand, even when the subject may be difficult to grasp, is one thing, but then to add the rider "otherwise they might turn and be forgiven" is quite something else. Did Jesus tell them stories to entertain while intending to keep them from seeing the truth? Did Jesus not want them to be forgiven? Surely not! So what else is at play on this occasion?

This is another situation where we need to differentiate between [a] what Jesus may have actually said, and [b] the time and context of the writer looking back with hindsight. I am certain that Jesus intended his parables and wisdom stories to help ordinary people seek and find the truth. Mark records here part of what Jesus is said to have taught that day [Mark 4:2]. It was the story of the farmer scattering seed, some of which fell along the path, and the birds came and ate it up. Other seed fell on thin soil that was full of stones. It did grow a little but without roots the plants simply withered and died when the sun came up. Thorn bushes choked the seed that fell among them. But other seed fell on good soil and not only did it grow but multiplied up to a hundred times more [Mark 4: 3-8].

It is a simple story told to people who worked the land. They knew that hand scattering seed would cause some to perish and some to grow. The message was simple: every action has an effect! This basic wisdom teaching can be developed so that, in the

Kingdom of God, all people are able to grow and thrive. However, life and personalities are such that some people will start the faith journey but then pull away when the going gets tough. They will never mature in the faith. This is where I think the story attributed to Jesus actually ended when he reminded them that those who had ears to hear, then make sure that you hear! [Mark 4:9]

In my opinion the addition of "they may be ever seeing but never perceiving, and ever hearing but never understanding; otherwise they might turn and be forgiven!" is a Peter/Mark hindsight comment as they struggled to understand why the ministry of Jesus was a failure in so many ways and for so many people. It is as though Peter and Mark were making excuses for the failure of Jesus to achieve what he had set out to do. For both of them this simple and yet profound teaching of Jesus failed, not because of anything that Jesus did or did not do, but because the listeners themselves failed to grasp the meaning of the message. The failure of the ministry of Jesus was placed into the hands of those who looked but could not see; those who listened but never understood.

"Whom shall I send? And who will go for us?"

Is this also another case of Midrash, taking an earlier story, especially one that would have been told in the cycle of synagogue readings and therefore known to the listeners, and applying it to the story of the farmer and the scattered seeds? It is, after all, a reference back to 1st Isaiah 6:1-13 where the prophet received his commission from God. In a vision Isaiah saw the temple and a heavenly host calling to one another and praising God. Isaiah then described something akin to a mighty earthquake that filled the temple with smoke. In fear, Isaiah realized the magnitude of his sin believing that he was standing in the presence of the Almighty. Then his fear was compounded as a seraph approached him with tongs bearing a hot coal from the fire. The seraph touched the coal on the lips of Isaiah and said to him, "Your guilt is taken away and your sin atoned for."

Then comes one of the images of the Hebrew Scriptures that

always thrills me: the Lord asked somewhat pointedly, "Whom shall I send? And who will go for us?"

I sometimes imagine 1st Isaiah standing on one leg, shuffling in embarrassment, and looking around to see if another human being was standing nearby – perhaps it was the other who would volunteer for this 'sending'? I do not think of Isaiah leaping in joy, like a child in kindergarten, hand waving in the air, "Teacher, choose me! Choose me!" In the story Isaiah had little choice, being the only human standing in the presence of the Lord and the heavenly host! More realistically, perhaps Isaiah whispered in such a low voice that the Lord had to lean forward, "What did you say? Speak up, man!" And a little louder this time, Isaiah reluctantly coughed out, "Here am I. Send me if you must."

But then there are the strange instructions that accompanied the Lord's commissioning of Isaiah:

> 9 He said, "Go and tell this people: 'Be ever hearing, but never understanding; be ever seeing, but never perceiving.' 10 Make the heart of this people calloused; make their ears dull and close their eyes. Otherwise they might see with their eyes, hear with their ears, understand with their hearts, and turn and be healed.
> (Isaiah 6 New International Version)

The Lord's commission was a statement of reproach and judgment for the sins of the people as a whole. When Isaiah asked the Lord how long this judgment would last the reply was: "Until the cities lie ruined and without inhabitant, until the houses are left deserted and the fields ruined and ravaged, until the LORD has sent everyone far away and the land is utterly forsaken. And though a tenth remains in the land, it will again be laid waste. But as the terebinth and oak leave stumps when they are cut down, so the holy seed will be the stump in the land."

Even though God's judgment would be calamitous for a while,

the great commission of 1st Isaiah ends with a clear statement that all is not lost and some "holy seed will be the stump in the land" that will grow again. This is what Peter and Mark were saying when they quoted 1st Isaiah 6: even though the ministry of Jesus appeared to have been a failure because the sinful people of God would not listen and respond, there would be a seed that would grow and therefore, in the longer term, all was not lost for God's people.

As for the desolation foreseen in the 1st Isaiah vision, perhaps this is the desolation in which Mark is writing? It could be the desolation of Rome burned to the ground and the persecution of Jew and Christian as Nero's punishment? Or perhaps Mark is writing just after the destruction of the Jerusalem Temple; but if so, then this would date the writing of Mark's Gospel as later rather than earlier [i.e. post rather than pre-70 CE].

There follows a story about light not being hidden and a reminder that the way in which one treats another is the way in which the other will respond – and sometimes worse [Mark 4:21-25]! But in the Mark account Jesus again returns to the theme of farmers and seeds [Mark 4:26-32].

Echoing the words of John Cage

I now reference the American composer, philosopher and writer, John Cage, famous (or infamous!) for his 1952 'musical composition' *4'33"*, 4 minutes and 33 seconds of silence. Cage once commented, "I can't understand why people are frightened by new ideas. I'm frightened of old ones."

John Cage died in 1992 but every Church and every Christian should welcome the wisdom of that statement. Without such an open and challenging attitude then I doubt that Christianity has a worthwhile future in our increasingly secular and industrialized age. There are many, but by no means all Christians who need certainty in an increasingly uncertain world and find it locked into a 'nothing changes here' attitude that seems to be endemic in much of the Christian Church. Other Christians, however, are walking away from the Christian Church often because they can no longer take the 'to be part of us you have to believe what we tell you' attitude.

As I write this book the latest national population Census figures available in Britain were gathered in 2001. That Census recorded a population of 59,300,000. It is estimated that the population of Britain is now around 61,000,000. According to the 2001 Census, 42,079,000 (that was 71.6% of the adult population) said that they considered themselves to be 'Christian'. However, between 1979 and 2005, half of all regular church attendees stopped going to church.

But both statistics and the Bible alike should never be taken at face value. Such a high response of 71.6% reflected a cultural understanding that Britain is 'a Christian country'. What this figure also represented was not just those who considered themselves to be 'Christian' but it also included those who wished to make the statement that they were not Muslim, Jew, Hindu and so on.

The far right British National Party gained seats in County Council and European elections in 2009. Its evil scare-mongering tactics proclaiming that Britain is being overtaken by migrants, and particularly by Muslims, are shown to be false. The percentages will doubtless change between 2001 and the next Census in 2011, but are we really under a Muslim siege? In 2001 the number of adherents of Islam came to just 1,546,626 or just 2.7% of the adult population! The number of people who said that they had no religion or refused to answer that particular question amounted to almost 23% of the population. So, as far as religion was concerned, in 2001 Christianity represented almost 75% of those who stated that they had some outward appearance of religious attachment. I await the publication of the 2011 national Census with interest.

However, we should not be fooled into thinking that association with Christianity meant participation in the life of the Church. The Census indicated that perhaps as much as 66% of the adult population had no active link with any religion, despite how they had responded on the Census forms. Religion in Britain, and not just Christianity, has suffered a colossal weakening since the 1950s, and all signs indicate an ongoing and systematic secularization of the general public. The same pattern is being experienced in other European countries and now across North America, even in the Bible Belt of the USA.

The more evangelical or literalist wing of the Christian Church blames the liberals and the progressives like me for this massive decline in Church attendance. The American Christian nationalists and Christian revisionists blame everyone but themselves, unwittingly looking to create in Christendom what has been created in Iran: theocracy in place of democracy! However, I am of the opinion that it is the exclusiveness, literalism and certainty that many of the Churches appear to preach in this increasingly secularized society (a society that rejects absolute answers and external authority) that have greatly contributed to the demise of the Church as a whole. So here is my appeal to all who remain in the church: I echo the words of John Cage: "I can't understand why people are frightened by new ideas. I'm frightened of old ones."

Parables concerning the planting of seed

It is in this same questioning Spirit that I find something else that intrigues me in the parable of the mustard seed: as I keep reminding people, Mark was the first Gospel in our canon of Scripture to have been written, so why did Matthew and then Luke, writing some 20 to 30 years later, ignore the first parable about seeds but include the parable of the mustard seed?

Both parables concern the planting and the growth of the seed. Both highlight the fact that it is from small beginnings that big things grow. Both emphasize that this growth happens organically and without our involvement, other than the original planting or scattering of the seeds. But the mustard seed parable ends with birds perching in the branches – a tranquil picture, but the other parable of the seeds finishes with the active cutting of the harvest corn. Why did Matthew and then Luke both choose to include the parable of the tree offering shade from the heat of the sun but ignore the story of taking a sickle to the harvest?

Again we need to remember the context in which the Gospels were written. Mark's Gospel reflects the memories and teaching of his mentor the Apostle Peter. Both Peter and Paul had recently been executed. It was the only Gospel to have been written during the Jewish rebellion against Roman occupation that began in 67 and ended with the mass suicide at Masada in 73. Things seemed bleak indeed for the Jewish and gentile followers of Jesus living in the Roman Empire at that time.

I am convinced that Mark was writing before that fateful destruction of the Jerusalem Temple. He looked for hope and he found it in believing that he and other followers of the Jesus Way were living in the end times when Jesus soon would return to judge the living and the dead. The returned Jesus would complete his previous earthly intention and bring their suffering to an end with the defeat of Rome.

Mark and his fellow Christians in Rome believed that Jesus had sown them like the seeds in the parables, and it was the work of God and not their own efforts that had brought them through thus far. They trusted God to keep them safe until the time when Jesus would come back. No matter how painful the interim may be, the sickle signaled the time of harvest. They would be reaped and taken home in glory to be with Jesus. For Peter/Mark, the Kingdom of God would come in all its glory as an end time event. They found support for this thinking in the book of Joel 3:12-14:

> 12Let the nations be roused; let them advance into the Valley of Jehoshaphat, for there I will sit to judge all the nations on every side. 13Swing the sickle, for the harvest is ripe. Come, trample the grapes, for the winepress is full and the vats overflow – so great is their wickedness! 14Multitudes, multitudes in the valley of decision! For the day of the LORD is near in the valley of decision. [New International Version)]

But the Gospels of Matthew and Luke were written some 10 years or more after the devastation that resulted from the Jewish rebellion against Rome. The rebellion had failed. The Temple in Jerusalem, the Shekinah, the place of meeting between the Lord God of the Jews and the Jewish people, had been destroyed. The Sadducees and the Priestly Temple Cult had gone forever. All this had happened and Jesus had not yet returned!

Neither Matthew nor Luke could take the same line as Peter/Mark and proclaim that the Roman persecution of Christians and the Roman occupation of the Jewish lands would be ended by the return of Jesus. It was too late and therefore Mark's reference to the sickle, the winepress and the judgment of God against Rome could no longer be sustained and it was quietly dropped from the Gospels of Matthew and Luke.

Yet there was comfort in the image of the mustard seed story of Mark. From the smallest seed grew the largest garden tree! In the heat of the day there was shelter. In the heat of life being lived under the brutality of Roman occupation, the followers of Jesus believed that they could find shade and protection in him. Even if their bodies were destroyed, life would continue through all eternity.

We need to be aware of at least three ancient texts that were read by Jew and gentile followers of Jesus to reassure them in their uncertain and dangerous times. These are really what the mustard seed stories were all about. Daniel 4:10-12 records the dream of King Nebuchadnezzar:

> 10These are the visions I saw while lying in bed: I looked, and there before me stood a tree in the middle of the land. Its height was enormous. 11The tree grew large and strong and its top touched the sky; it was visible to the ends of the earth. 12 Its leaves were beautiful, its fruit abundant, and on it was food for all. Under it the wild animals found shelter, and the birds lived in its branches; from it every creature was fed. [New International Version]

But as reassuring as these verses may have been, there was an even deeper subtext: when putting these verses into the context of Daniel Chapter 4 one can see that the whole chapter is one of judgment of the Lord God of the Jews against King Nebuchadnezzar. Although the Book of Daniel was not written down until around 165 years before Jesus, it referred back to earlier persecutions, military occupations and exiles that had taken place between the 8th and 6th centuries before Jesus.

Surely it was no accident that Mark, Matthew and Luke all referenced this Daniel passage that told of the days of the persecution of the Jewish forefathers. It told of the 6th century exile and captivity in Babylon while others remained under Babylonian occupation in their conquered and defeated land. Perhaps both Matthew and Luke were including the coded subtext that what had happened to Babylon would eventually, by the grace and sovereignty of the Lord God of the Jewish Christians, happen to the Romans who were persecuting them at that time?

A second reference for Mark, Matthew and Luke was Ezekiel 17:22-24, written again during the 6th century Babylonian Exile:

> [22]This is what the Sovereign LORD says: I myself will take a shoot from the very top of a cedar and plant it; I will break off a tender sprig from its topmost shoots and plant it on a high and lofty mountain. [23]On the mountain heights of Israel I will plant it; it will produce branches and bear fruit and become a splendid cedar. Birds of every kind will nest in it; they will find shelter in the shade of its branches. [24]All the trees of the forest will know that I the LORD bring down the tall tree and make the low tree grow tall. I dry up the green tree and make the dry tree flourish. 'I the LORD have spoken, and I will do it.'
> (New International Version)

Here is the reassurance that no matter how difficult things were under

Roman occupation, the Sovereign Lord God of Israel previously had brought the people out of captivity and into freedom, and the same would happen again with the inevitable defeat of Rome. What greater encouragement could there be than to be confidently told, "I the LORD have spoken, and I will do it"?

A third reference is also in Ezekiel Chapter 31, the wonderful imagery of verses 2 to 9:

> [2]Son of man, say to Pharaoh king of Egypt and to his hordes: "Who can be compared with you in majesty? [3]Consider Assyria, once a cedar in Lebanon, with beautiful branches overshadowing the forest; it towered on high, its top above the thick foliage. [4]The waters nourished it, deep springs made it grow tall; their streams flowed all around its base and sent their channels to all the trees of the field. [5]So it towered higher than all the trees of the field; its boughs increased and its branches grew long, spreading because of abundant waters. [6]All the birds of the sky nested in its boughs, all the animals of the wild gave birth under its branches; all the great nations lived in its shade. [7]It was majestic in beauty, with its spreading boughs, for its roots went down to abundant waters. [8]The cedars in the garden of God could not rival it, nor could the junipers equal its boughs, nor could the plane trees compare with its branches – no tree in the garden of God could match its beauty. [9]I made it beautiful with abundant branches, the envy of all the trees of Eden in the garden of God. (New International Version)

Again, in the context of the whole chapter, this is another story of reassurance for the followers of Jesus that judgment would be heaped upon their Roman oppressors.

So, do you interpret the two stories of the seeds contained in Mark's Gospel as simple agricultural stories about sowing, growing and reaping with all the old traditional answers given by preachers down the years? Or dare you ask the questions, "What else may have been in the coded subtext? What else was not only written on the line, but what was written between the lines and behind the lines?" And, no matter how we interpret these parables, the most important questions of all are these:

- "What does all this mean for you and for me in the daily life and context of here and now?"

- "How does this relate to what you and I have to deal with day by day?"

- "What do these stories say to you and me today?"

Considering the 2001 Census I am convinced that the face value old ways of interpreting the Scriptures have contributed greatly to the massive decline in Church attendance. Therefore I am certain that we need to take sacred risks in challenging traditional ideas so that the Church may have a future. Again I echo the words of John Cage: "I can't understand why people are frightened by new ideas. I'm frightened of old ones."

According to the narrative, at the end of the day teaching from the deck of the boat to the hordes on the shore, Jesus said to his disciples, "Let us go over to the other side." As they started the crossing the Sea of Galilee Jesus, exhausted from his day of teaching, fell asleep in the stern of the boat. All of a sudden an angry storm began to blow and waves broke over the sides of the boat and it began to sink. Somewhat terrified the disciples woke Jesus and in fear, or may be in rebuke, called above the sound of the howling wind and crashing waves, "Teacher, don't you care if we drown?"

In the story, Jesus stood and called to the wind and the waves, "Quiet! Be still!" The storm ceased and Jesus turned to his disciples and asked a very strange question, "Why are you so afraid? Do you still have no faith?"

Mark's story [4:35-41] misses out a hugely important conversation that I am sure took place on the boat: "What do you mean, 'Why are you afraid'? Look what we've just been through? We could have been drowned, and where would that have got us?"

But Mark has sanitized Peter's memories and he simply records:

> 41They were terrified and asked each other, "Who is this? Even the wind and the waves obey him!"
> [Mark 4:41 (New International Version)]

Mark Chapter 5:
The nature of faith, unbelief and the impact upon the training of the Disciples

This chapter begins with the arrival of Jesus and the disciples on the other side of the Sea of Galilee. This story has already been addressed in Chapter 2 of this book in the context of exploring the Gospels as social commentary, so we now move to consider a dead girl and a sick woman [Mark 5:21-43]. Jesus had returned to the boat and crossed back to the Capernaum shore. Before he landed another large crowd had gathered and among them was Jairus, the very distressed ruler of the synagogue. As Jesus stepped ashore Jairus fell at his feet and implored Jesus to accompany him to his home because his daughter was dying. Jairus obviously believed that the child's last chance of life was the healing touch of Jesus. Jairus led the way through the crowd, and Jesus and his disciples followed him.

But as the crowd pressed in on Jesus there was a sick woman who had been made penniless by the failure of doctors to heal her of twelve years of bleeding, and still the situation worsened for her. She had heard about Jesus and of some of those who had been healed by him. This woman, almost as a last attempt to be made well, made it her mission to touch the hem of the cloak worn by Jesus. Her one thought was that to touch even the hem would be sufficient to heal her.

Now that was faith – anticipating what will be and accepting it as already having happened. She pushed through the crowd, got within touching distance and thrust out an arm. She touched the hem. Not only did she know that her bleeding had ceased but she was convinced that she was completely and instantaneously healed.

According to the story it was at that moment, within the entire crowd all jostling and reaching out to touch him, that this fleeting contact from the sick woman alerted Jesus to power going from him. Jesus stopped and turned around to face the crowd beside and behind him and asked, "Who touched my clothes?"

His disciples dismissed the comment with a wry smile. "Look at all these people! They are all touching you. We are fighting a way through so that you can follow Jairus. Come quickly. The little girl is dying."

Jesus stood still and asked again, "Who touched my clothes?" The woman knew that she had no choice but to own up. It was in fear and with great trembling that she fell on her knees in front of Jesus and told him the why and wherefore of having touched him. "I am sick of being sick. I have spent all my money on useless doctors. You were my last chance and you have healed me!"

Jesus did not preach a sermon. He did not tell another story for the crowd to hear and to be amazed. He simply helped the woman to her feet and said that it was her faith, not an external intervention by Yahweh God or by anyone else that had healing power: "Daughter, your faith has healed you. Go in peace and be freed from your suffering."

However, in spending these few moments with the sick woman who would now go on her way rejoicing, the cost was apparently greater for Jairus. Even as Jesus was telling the woman that her faith had healed her, men from the house of Jairus arrived with the news that his daughter had died. Jesus had not got there quick enough.

Jairus must have been devastated. Even if he did not say it, surely the thoughts went through his head? "Jesus, you healed a woman but you let my daughter die. The woman has had a longer life. My daughter had her whole life ahead of her. Why did you stop and heal the woman and let my daughter die? Where's the justice in all of that? Life just isn't fair!" These are the questions that those of us who minister to others at times of bereavement often have to face.

But Jesus ignored these bringers of bad tidings and turned to Jairus and said, "Don't be afraid. Be like that woman – her faith has healed her. If you have similar faith then your daughter is not dead, only sleeping!"

Jesus took Peter, James and John the brother of James with

him and they followed Jairus to his home. When they arrived the professional wailing was under way.

"Why all this commotion and wailing? The child is not dead but asleep."

At which point the wailing turned to mocking laughter of Jesus. He told the wailers to leave but took the young girl's mother and father and the three disciples with him to the lifeless body. Jesus took her hand and said to her, "Little girl, I say to you, get up!"

I cannot explain such things. I have heard claims of such death to life happenings among the Pentecostals and especially the television evangelists. I have no wish to undermine such claims but all I can say is that I have never witnessed raising the dead and therefore it is beyond my comprehension. However, in the narrative, as soon as Jesus had spoken, this young twelve-year-old girl immediately stood up and walked around. Not surprisingly all who witnessed this were astonished.

"Don't tell anyone about this – not even in this synagogue where my ministry, my disciples and I all have been welcomed," Jesus said. "And don't just stand there with your mouths open, welcome the girl back to life and give her something to eat! She must be starving!"

In my imagination and experience, Jesus was never a 'goody two shoes' who only spoke in Gospel language. He was a man of the streets – a man of the earth, so full of humanity and laughter. He was a real man with whom all who wanted could know that they were in the presence of the sacred.

I long for people to come afresh to the Bible and to read it enthusiastically as a dynamic life-changing book. Remember that in Mark's Gospel the story of the healing of these two comes immediately after Jesus had stilled the storm at sea. Mark has Jesus demonstrating power over the natural world as well as over life and death.

Now, to ask if Jesus really woke up from his sleep in a storm-tossed boat and ordered the storm to cease, and it obeyed his command; or whether or not Jesus had healed the hemorrhaging woman and raised to new life the 12-year-old girl who had died – this is to ask the wrong questions. Whether these did or did not happen is not really a question that is worth pondering. What is important is to ask two other questions:

"How was Mark's Gospel influenced by his social, political and religious contexts when he recorded this story?" and again, "What does Mark's account say to us today?"

This is yet another of those situations where we need to differentiate between [a] what Jesus perhaps actually said and did, and [b] the time and context of the writer looking back with hindsight. I again repeat myself but we must never forget that Mark was writing in Rome during the 7th decade persecution of those associated with the Jewish synagogues – including the Jewish and gentile followers of Jesus. But Mark was also recording events that had supposedly happened more than 30 years before, not in Rome but in Roman-occupied Palestine. Spong helpfully invites us to consider Mark's approach to telling his miracle stories in that they tended to follow a set pattern:

- A difficulty to be defeated by Jesus.

- The action of Jesus that ends in success.

- Confirmation that it was Jesus who had achieved the desired outcome.

Think again about the storm on the Sea of Galilee. The difficulty is the storm itself. The action of Jesus is to demand that the storm stops. The confirmation is that the disciples were amazed that even the winds and the waves obeyed him.

A hemorrhaging woman and a young girl

Or think of the two other stories: the first being the difficulty of a hemorrhaging woman who has spent all her money on doctors and still the problem worsens. The action of Jesus is that, even though he does not know who has drawn power from him, by touching the hem of his garment the woman is healed. The confirmation is that Jesus turns and asks who touched him and received power from him. The woman owns up and all recognize that Jesus has God's power and he offers God's healing peace in spite of the Jewish Law of *niddah*.

Menstrual bleeding was and remains, for Orthodox Jews, unclean and anyone either touching or being touched by a menstruating woman was also made unclean. Leviticus 15:19 states: "A woman who has a flow of blood in her body shall be a *'niddah'* for seven days, and all who touch her shall be ritually impure until sundown."

Again, the next story in this section by Mark involves the difficulty of a 12-year-old girl who dies while waiting for Jesus to come to heal her. The action of Jesus is to say that the dead girl is not dead but sleeping – and the onlookers laugh at him. The confirmation is that it is Jesus who takes the girl, sits her up and restores her to life to the astonishment of everyone.

You may well ask, "So what?" The 'so what' for me is that Mark is telling his miracle stories according to a literary formula that does not require that the stories be historically true [*mythos*], although they may well have happened [*logos*]. But there is so much more to the story of the hemorrhaging woman and the young girl. Notice the following historical coincidences – or is it merely another example of Mark's literary style of telling a good story?

Both stories concern female suffering. Both stories center on Jesus telling the woman and the father of the young girl to have faith and to trust in God. Both stories use the number '12' – the woman's hemorrhage was probably continuous menstrual bleeding that had lasted 12 years, and the young girl was 12 years old, about the time that a young girl commenced her regular cycle of periods. [In passing I reference a comment from my mentor Brian Wilson who said to me that he felt that I was taking my example of '12' a little too far especially when considering the type of diet available in those days that may have delayed the onset of puberty by some years. Be that as it may, I contend that Mark was really making menstruation a link between the hemorrhaging woman and the 12-year-old girl.]

Also it is important to notice that a menstruating woman touched Jesus and therefore he was made ritually unclean. But according to Mark, Jesus did not make a fuss about it but appeared to ignore the ancient Law of *niddah* as he treated the woman as an equal, no longer made impure by the natural cycles of life. And if the 12-year-old girl was also entering puberty and beginning to menstruate then Jesus also was made ritually unclean by taking her hand.

There is another connection with '12': it was God's choice that there had been twelve tribes of Israel; it was the choice of Jesus that there were twelve close disciples. Twelve was a number associated with God's acceptance. And within a society where women were socially unimportant possessions of father or husband, Mark has Jesus affirming that women were just as acceptable to God as were the men. This was radical political and cultural teaching by Jesus and experienced by the early Peter community. To get behind the Scriptures in this way can give a whole new understanding of the importance that Jesus placed upon women.

What a message for women in the world today – that they are respected and accepted as sacred equals to men and that the natural cycles of life do not diminish them or make them inferior or ritually unclean. Just think how this radical Jesus who accepted women as more than unclean could not only liberate women but could re-educate men in their attitudes towards women!

Mark Chapter 6:
Jesus visits his original hometown

According to the narrative, for the first time, Jesus departed Capernaum and travelled back to his hometown of Nazareth [Mark 6:1-6]. His disciples accompanied him on that 20-mile walk. People then gathered in the Nazareth synagogue on the Sabbath to listen to his teaching, and many were amazed and puzzled. "Where did this man get these things? What's this wisdom that has been given him, that he even does miracles!"

But then amazement changed to incredulity, "Isn't this the carpenter? Isn't this Mary's son and the brother of James, Joseph, Judas and Simon? Aren't his sisters here with us?"

Mark then records that the local people who had grown up with Jesus among them, playing as any child played, destined to follow his father into the carpenter's workshop, took offence at Jesus and his teaching.

Jesus said to them, "Only in his hometown, among his relatives and in his own house is a prophet without honor."

There were many followers of Jesus at the beginning of his ministry who saw him as wisdom teacher and miracle worker. Some then slowly began to see him as a prophet. But others, especially those of his family and those who lived in his hometown, rejected him. The more that Jesus began to break the Laws as interpreted by the Pharisees and the Sadducees the more the spiritual leadership began to see him as a threat and as a heretic.

Although Mark's was the original Gospel as far as the Canon of Christian Scripture is concerned, and Thomas has but one saying [32] related to this story, I prefer Luke's expansive additions to the story of the return of Jesus to Nazareth [Luke 4:14-30]. Unlike Mark's account, following his baptism by John and the sojourn in the desert, Luke records that Jesus went straight back to the villages of Galilee. He preached in the power of the Spirit, and news was quickly transmitted through the towns and villages. Luke says that wherever he went, Jesus taught in their synagogues to the praise of the people. But all that changed when Jesus reached the Nazareth synagogue. It was here that Jesus, as a young child, would have been nurtured and taught the Law and the Prophets of the Hebrew Scriptures.

The scroll of the Prophets

From the Gospels it appears that it was the custom of Jesus to attend synagogue as any faithful Jew would have done, just as it was the custom to read the whole of the Torah and other selected passages from the Prophets, over an annual cycle. According to Luke's additions to the Peter/Mark story, on that particular Sabbath it was the turn of Isaiah [Chapter 61] to be read as the Haftorah scroll (i.e. the scroll of the Prophets).

The scroll Jesus was offered contained the words attributed to the prophet Isaiah. Jesus stood up, walked to the reading desk and took the reading pointer so that he would not hand touch the scroll. The Haftorah scroll was unrolled until he came to a particular point and he began to read:

> 1The Spirit of the Sovereign LORD is on me, because the LORD has anointed me to proclaim good news to the poor. He has sent me to bind up the brokenhearted, to proclaim freedom for the captives and release from darkness for the prisoners, 2to proclaim the year of the LORD's favor and the day of vengeance of our God, to comfort all who mourn. [Isaiah 61:1-2 (New International Version)]

The people who were listening were quite content with the reading. I can imagine the satisfaction and the quiet enthusiasm beginning to bubble around the synagogue: little verbal asides, heads nodding and smiles all round.

"This is Joseph's son – and we've heard stories of wonderful things that he has said and done as he has travelled through Galilee on his way to us – to us!"

And another little aside from neighbor to neighbor: "Jesus is one of our own – one of us!"

The local baker may have turned to the innkeeper and whispered, "If Jesus remains in Nazareth then his ministry will grow and we can bask in his glory!"

"Yes," smiled the innkeeper. "We will receive the shekels of the generated commerce from those who will come to listen and to be healed. After all, they will need bread to eat and somewhere to sleep at night."

As I understand it, the synagogue custom was that the reader of the Haftorah scroll would then sit down and begin to speak. But things started to go wrong and the warning bells began to ring when Jesus rolled up the scroll, gave it back to the synagogue attendant and sat down. Everyone watched and listened. He simply said to them, "Today this Scripture is fulfilled in your hearing."

It was blasphemy to claim that he was the one to fulfill the Isaiah Scripture that he had just read to them. It only got worse when Jesus took examples from the history of the Jewish people and pointed out that God did not always heal or appear to care for Jewish widows or lepers, but sometimes, during the times of Elijah and Elisha, God chose to heal foreigners, those who the Jews thought were beyond the care of Yahweh God because, they believed, only the Jews were the chosen children of Yahweh.

Here, early on in Luke's Gospel, we find Luke's experience of Jesus beginning to be demonstrated in a broad vision of Yahweh's concern for all people. This was Judaism's religious barrier of that time and the gentile outsider, Luke, has Jesus attacking it, pointing out that Jews were not the only ones to be blessed by God. And the result was that the people in the synagogue were filled with anger and they tried to take Jesus to throw him off the cliff to kill him.

Considering Isaiah 61

But we cannot progress beyond this point in Luke's account of the Peter/Mark story of Jesus being rejected by his family and hometown friends without further considering Isaiah 61. What was Jesus saying that he had come to fulfill?

Jesus was saying that he had been anointed by God to preach good news to the poor. So who were the poor? All those who were not in league with the Roman oppressors, especially the rural peasants to whom Jesus mainly ministered. Jesus, an ordinary carpenter who may have become a rabbi, had acquired sufficient skills that enabled him to read the Isaiah Scripture that Sabbath day. Here he was among his own people saying that he was the one of whom Isaiah 61 had spoken some six centuries before. And what good news might the poor have wanted to hear?

- That there is an alternative to the oppression of Rome!

- That there will come a time when adequate food will be on every table!

- That there will be a fair share of all God's good gifts!

- That God did not love the healthy, the rich and the important more than God loved the sick, the poor and the unimportant!

What good news that must have been to the downtrodden poor and oppressed! So why were they filled with so much anger that they tried to take Jesus to kill him?

But the Gospels go on to make clear that Jesus did not just speak the words of universal and compassionate agape love – he lived his message and broke the barriers that divided. Jesus ate with publicans and sinners, with those who were the outcasts and dregs of society. Jesus healed the Roman centurion's child, an enemy of the Jews. Jesus talked with the Samaritan woman at the well, breaking the taboos of a man not talking to an unaccompanied adult female, and of a Jew talking with the hated and despised Samaritans.

Jesus even told the story of the Good Samaritan, praising this despised man for doing the very things that the Jewish priests and leaders should have done but who had allowed religion and fear to get in the way. Jesus touched the blind and the lame. Jesus touched the untouchables – the lepers so that they all could be healed and restored. That was the impact of Jesus. That was the power of the compassionate agape love of Jesus that created and maintained the life of the early churches – words of wisdom lived out in practical ways long after the Calvary execution.

Jesus went on and said that God had sent him "to proclaim freedom for the prisoners and to release the oppressed…" So who were the prisoners and the oppressed? They included those who were in the prison of personal debt, and even the slavery of Jew enslaved to Jew. They were those who were exploited by the Sadducees in the Temple and cruelly treated by the Roman occupiers. Jesus was condemning the corruption of God's love that denied all people justice and their God-given share of God's abundance. Surely that was good news to the downtrodden poor and oppressed. That again was the impact of Jesus. That was the power that created and maintained the life of the early churches – words of wisdom lived out in practical ways. No wonder the religious leaders, Herod Antipas and the Roman oppressors wanted him dead; but why were ordinary people, those just like Jesus, filled with so much anger that they tried to kill him? Jesus said that God had sent him "to proclaim the year of the Lord's favor." [See Appendix Six for examples of this Jesus agape love as applying to life today.]

Do you remember the American politician Barry Goldwater? He became the Republican Party's presidential nominee in July 1964. In his acceptance speech he said two things – the first with which I profoundly disagree: "I would remind you that extremism in the defense of liberty is no vice." But to the second I give unreserved support – and it sums up the core issue of this part of this book: "Moderation in the pursuit of justice is no virtue."

Without an idea, nothing will change. But a good idea without action will change nothing. One of the most telling invitations made by Jesus is applicable to each of us: to live the message, to go that extra mile, to go and do the same as Jesus had done. So we should not be those who just talk about the wisdom and social justice concerns of Jesus. It is my contention that we should live these concerns for God's sake, for our sake, for the sake of people living in hell today, and for the sake of generations still to come.

So why were the ordinary people in that Nazareth synagogue filled with so much anger that they tried to take Jesus to throw him off the cliff to kill him? It is conjecture on my part but I suspect that it was because they were blinded by their strict adherence to the formulaic and traditional teaching of the synagogue and Temple leaders and rulers. These ordinary people were taught in such a way that they had become slaves to religion when the message of Jesus was to make religion serve ordinary people. Has anything changed in the ecclesiastical world today?

Jesus franchises his ministry

Returning to Mark's Gospel and we find the story moving to Jesus franchising his ministry so that the disciples could continue the work even if Jesus himself was thrown off the cliff or killed in some other way. This has been mentioned earlier in this book by referencing Crossan's point that John the Baptist monopolized and centered the ministry upon himself, so that when he was executed the ministry ceased.

But the disciples of Jesus returned with stories of successful ministry. As if to contrast the work of John the Baptist and Jesus of Nazareth, Peter/Mark then went into a long explanation as to what had happened to John [Mark 6:14-29].

> On his birthday Herod gave a banquet for his high officials and military commanders and the leading men of Galilee. [22]When the daughter of Herodias came in and danced, she pleased Herod and his dinner guests. The king said to the girl, "Ask me for anything you want, and I'll give it to you."

> [23]And he promised her with an oath, "Whatever you ask I will give you, up to half my kingdom." [24]She went out and said to her mother, "What shall I ask for?"
> "The head of John the Baptist," she answered.
> [Mark 6:21-24 (New International Version)]

What a gruesome and unpleasant story this is! What on earth is the message that we are meant to interpret concerning the bizarre execution of John the Baptist? Also, why did Mark include this particular weird episode in his narrative, and why at this point in his version of the Jesus story? It seems totally out of place. Not that it matters, but in my opinion it would have been better positioned right back in Chapter 1 verse 14 where we read "After John was arrested… " But Mark chose to continue Chapter 1:14 with the statement that Jesus went to Galilee and continued to tell the good news.

Some passages of Scripture are easily explored and developed by the preacher, but this is not one of them. When I turned to my bookshelf in search of the wisdom of my usual mentors – the new Trinity of Borg, Crossan and Spong – I discovered that all of them seem to ignore this passage. They often reference the stories on either side, but this one is a non-starter as far as they are concerned. There were odd references that came to nothing and on the whole this passage is of little interest to our popular progressive writers and thinkers. So in my search for understanding I ask a number of questions about this passage.

Is it a story about a foolish king who is so besotted with his new wife Herodias and her young daughter that he made a rash promise that he would give anything that the daughter requested, even up to half his kingdom?

When the request came for the head of John the Baptist, was the King more concerned for his own honor than he was interested in the life of his prisoner?

Would the King not go back on his word for fear that he would lose face among the gathered dignitaries?

What a hideous and sordid story this is in which one man's high opinion of himself, his power and his privilege resulted in the death of a courageous man!

Or was it a story of the struggle between power and popularity? John the Baptist had quite a following among ordinary folk and he had the courage to speak up for what he thought was right. This included vocal opposition and condemnation of the puppet regime of Herod Antipas. But what John lacked was the power of the elite. Maybe the King would have moved against John the Baptist and silenced him earlier if it had not been for the size of his following among the general public? Perhaps this is why Mark included this repulsive and distasteful story in Chapter 6 and not Chapter 1, because, at this time in the developing ministry of Jesus, his growing popularity among the general public was similarly beginning to worry the King?

Perhaps a short while after the execution of John the Baptist, Herod was again challenged when he heard of the growing popularity of Jesus of Nazareth. Even more so when the common people began to talk of him as a miracle worker, wisdom teacher and prophet – even as Elijah or John the Baptist raised from the dead. Herod's response was that John, the man whom he had beheaded, had been raised from the dead. This was not so much a religious comment but an exasperated "Here we go again – now for my sake as a puppet of Rome, and for the peace of the people, Jesus will have to go the way of John the Baptist!"

Or perhaps, once again, this is a story of creative parallels where we need to differentiate between [a] what Jesus may have said, and [b] the time and context of the writer looking back with hindsight. Perhaps Mark's narrative was intended to remind his readers and listeners that what had happened to John the Baptist also happened to Jesus of Nazareth, and had, even more recently, happened to Peter and to Paul in Rome?

Note the constant parallel: all had been executed by the powers of the time. Perhaps Mark was also making the point that a similar fate awaited many followers of the Jesus Way? I remind you again that Mark's Gospel was probably written in Rome during a blood-spattered persecution of synagogue members, both Jew and gentile, including those Jews who accepted the witness of Jesus and those who rejected it. Remember also that Mark was writing near the beginning of the fateful Jewish rebellion against Roman occupation that saw the destruction of the Jerusalem Temple in 70 CE and the mass suicide of the remaining Jewish fighters at Masada in 73 CE. Was Mark reminding his readers and listeners of the cost of discipleship in taking on the powers that be?

So what may be the message of that same eternal Namaste Spirit to us at this moment through this dreadful and obnoxious story of the execution of John the Baptist? I cannot answer that for you but I encourage you not to dismiss this story but to engage with it and in your imagination become the oppressed John the Baptist, but also become the oppressor King Herod.

As you further engage with the story, be aware of the turnaround in the fortunes of what developed as the Christian Church. Its embryonic pre-Church leadership of John the Baptist and Jesus of Nazareth, along with its leadership in the early years of the formation of the Church, Paul of Tarsus, Peter of Capernaum and Mary of Magdala, all but Mary were executed because they dared to challenge and to subvert the political, religious and social order of their day. Perhaps the Eternal Spirit is saying to us that today the Christian Church spends too much of its time upholding and defending its political and social privilege at the cost of its true mission of social justice and prophetic service?

Before the arrival of Emperor Constantine in the early 4th century, the Christian communities were small-scattered groups on the edge of society. I contend that the Church lost its way when it allowed itself to be taken into the center of Roman Empirical power and privilege where its doctrines were formulated to reflect those issues of Empire, and where its dissenters and their Scriptures were destroyed.

Perhaps the story of the execution of John the Baptist is a Spirit-filled alarm bell appealing to the Church in the industrialized world to stop complaining that it is losing its voice and its influence in our increasingly and aggressively secular society, and to return to its calling to live the social justice of the Kingdom in the present? Perhaps the eternal Spirit is calling the Church in Britain to renounce its privilege and status in the House of Lords, the Second Chamber of Parliament, and to return to where it belongs, on the edge of power structures and living in the gutters alongside the poor and the powerless, exercising the most potent weapon of all, the power of the compassion and perfect love that is God?

I do not want to personify the eternal Namaste Spirit or to attribute to it human characteristics, but just suppose that the eternal Spirit is capable of shedding tears: how great would be the flood at the actions of the Fellowship of Confessing Anglicans and of the Bishop of Rochester, the Right Reverend Michael Nazir-Ali, who as recently as 2009 told the Sunday Telegraph that homosexuals should "repent and be changed."

Where is the power of the compassion and perfect love that is God in the splitting of the Episcopal Church in the United States? Where is that same compassion and perfect love that is squaring up for a colossal and destructive fight between the traditionalists and the reforming liberals in the Church of England?

I am a Methodist and we have our own opportunities, problems and challenges as witnessed in our annual Conferences. Methodists certainly know how to argue with Methodists! Although I do not speak with an official British Methodist voice, there is a question that ordinary Methodists often ask beneath their breath concerning the Anglican Methodist Covenant that was signed in London in November 2003: "With which Anglican Church will we be in Covenant when compassion and perfect love have been crushed under the might of the contenders for the soul and the future of Anglicanism?"

There are just two more related questions at this moment concerning the story of the execution of John the Baptist: what may the story of the execution of John the Baptist be saying to each of us concerning:

• The cost of doing what we, as individuals and as a Church community, believe is right as we attempt to live the presence of the Kingdom here and now?

• The cost of the insignificant small fry such as us maintaining the courage to follow the ways of Jesus as we take on the powerful big fish – business or ecclesiastical or political – as we put truth before tradition, and social justice between self-interest?

The feeding of the 5000

But we return again to the mythos story of the feeding of the 5000 [Mark 6:30-44]. In my understanding, this story points us to the nature of the Kingdom of Heaven. It had meaning then to the original listeners and readers of Mark's Gospel. But the nature of the mythos is that it has meaning for me in my present experience. I therefore begin with Mark 6:42 and 43, "They all ate and were satisfied, and the disciples picked up twelve basketfuls of broken pieces of bread and fish."

The context of this incident is important and all four of the Gospels in our canon of Scripture tell this story of the feeding of the 5000. Notice, however, that in all but John's Gospel the story follows immediately after the execution of John the Baptist.

As soon as Jesus heard that John the Baptist was dead, Jesus tried to escape from his following crowds. According to the narrative Jesus crossed to the eastern side of Lake Galilee presumably to have some peace and quiet both to mourn the loss of his friend and earlier mentor, and to think through how his own ministry may best develop: simply to take up the message of John the Baptist, 'Repent and be baptized' or to develop something radically different, perhaps

'What it means to live the Kingdom of Heaven in the present time?' Unfortunately the crowds who had witnessed Jesus healing the sick did not respect his need for solitude and they followed him across the Lake. They wanted to see and to experience more of what this man was doing. Surely, this is the mark of any true ministry – always having time for others, and especially for those in need. This applies to both clergy and laity!

The day progressed and evening approached. The crowds were still with Jesus and it would soon become too late in the day for them to safely find local villages where they could buy food. The crowd wanted to stay, even though they seemed to have no food, and Jesus continued to have compassion upon them and to heal them – wholeness and well-being were more important than missing the odd meal!

The disciples of Jesus went to him and pleaded with him to stop what he was doing and to send the crowds away so that they could find local villages where they might be able to buy food. Jesus then turned the tables on the disciples, perhaps because their request seemed to lack compassion? Jesus replied, "They don't have to leave. Why don't you give them something to eat?"

The disciples replied with some astonishment, "That would take eight months of a man's wages! Are we to go and spend that much on bread and give it to them to eat?"

[There are inconsistencies between the various Gospel accounts of this response by the disciples. For more details see Appendix Seven.]

These Gospel writers were not creating a story to be read or interpreted literally. They were not telling their hearers and readers that Jesus took 5 loaves and 2 fish and actually turned them into thousands of loaves and fishes. They were talking more about the impact of Jesus upon the crowds as he gave of his time, his charisma, his healing gifts and his wisdom. The Gospel writers were explaining in the best way that they could that such living is Kingdom of Heaven social justice living, and it causes others to open their spiritual eyes and to begin Kingdom of Heaven living as well.

The people saw how Jesus gave of himself unreservedly, unconditionally and sacrificially at a time when Jesus himself was seeking solitude – and they responded by opening themselves to begin to be more generous with the little that they had. They began to share so that all received and much was left over.

Now I am sure that, human nature being as incomplete as it is, some people that day abused the generosity and took more than their fair share. However, the evidence of the stories is that most people responded to the generosity of Jesus by being more generous themselves. Many obviously had more than enough food with them, and some had little or no food. But as sharing started, perhaps prompted by a small boy, people offered what they had to those around them who were in need of food. [See Appendix Eight for a fictional story that illustrates the practical message of this story.]

The real miracle was not a conjuring trick in which Jesus created food out of nothing. The real miracle was that even though they were not as fully human as the Spirit encouraged them to be (and encourages us in the same way), generosity breeds generosity, and compassion breeds compassion. It was true at the time of Jesus just as it is true for us today.

In saying this elsewhere I have been accused of watering down the Gospels and that this approach to the feeding of the 5000 not only lessens the miracle but it also lessens the idea of the God who intervenes in the natural laws to bless the chosen. Be that as it may, to see the real miracle in this story is to watch the people responding to Jesus by acting with greater humanity to those in need.

We miss so much of the presence of the Kingdom of Heaven because we too often over-spiritualize the stories or tend to look for the presence of the Namaste God in the big events of life, and in the perceived actions of the interventionist-type of superhuman being from somewhere 'out there'. In doing so we miss the miracle of perfect love indwelling us and coming to us in the ordinariness of our daily lives. It is as we live compassionately, so we will experience the compassionate presence of the Kingdom of Heaven.

I continue to push along with this idea because it is vital to my understanding of the Kingdom of God here and now. Let me ask, "Which is more powerful and of greater compassion, for me to sit back and to look on this incident of the feeding of the 5000 in terms of a heavenly conjuring trick for which I sing self-indulgent songs of praise to the interventionist God residing somewhere out there? Or is the power, the compassion and the miracle in this story for each one of us, as incomplete as we are, to realize that by living the social justice agenda and values of the Kingdom of Heaven here and now, the hungry are given something to eat; the thirsty are given something to drink; the strangers are truly welcomed; the naked are given clothes to wear; the sick are taken care of; the prisoners are visited?"

The answers to the needs of humanity, especially the eradicating of global poverty, are in the miracle that you and I have the sacred power to make all things new for all people. We can change our little bit of the world as we live the presence of the Kingdom of Heaven here and now. If enough of us around the world could abandon the theology that says, "God will take care of it, leave it to Him," and accept our responsibility to share what we have with those who have little, then the world will be fed and there will still be baskets of scraps left over.

What is needed is both the political will among those who control the international power and the international purse strings, and our commitment to live as Jesus lived. But sadly the collapse in 2008, the 7th year of the Doha Talks on a new global agreement to eradicate poverty, and the failure of the Copenhagen Climate Change Conference in December 2009 both demonstrated that the political will is not yet present among those who have the real international power.

I make no apology for reminding people again and again that the ways of the Kingdom of Heaven are the ways of living compassionately, sacrificially and unconditionally.

Surely, the true miracle of the story of the feeding of the 5000 is what the theology of Incarnation – of God with us – is all about? Such incarnational love was, and continues to be, completely revealed in the life and death of Jesus of Nazareth. It is this Jesus who is my Gateway to that incarnational reality of the Namaste Spirit indwelling all people. The true miracle of this story is that within the, as yet, incomplete human spirit, enlivened by the Namaste Jesus Spirit, there is the hope that can and will change things for the better for all people. In doing so, a new world will emerge and a better world will be created for us, for our children, for our grandchildren and for the generations still to come. In my developing understanding and experience, this is the reformation purpose of the good news of Jesus.

There are more mythos miracle stories and Kingdom teaching still to come. Again it is important that we understand the background to the miracle stories of feeding thousands, of storms on the sea, of withering fig trees, and so on. We cannot progress through Mark's Gospel without spending a little more time considering these issues.

We continue an exploration of the wonderful stories of the feeding of the 5000 and of Jesus walking on the water in Mark 6:30-56. According to the narrative this exploration continues with Jesus and 5000 men, plus their wives and children, somewhere on the fertile Plain of Gennesaret. This Plain was approximately five miles long and two miles wide, along the northwest shore of the Sea of Galilee. It is possible that the more specific geographic setting of the story of this extraordinary feeding 'miracle' was at Tabgha, two miles down the shore from Capernaum. I say this because Tabgha is the time-honored setting for several events in the ministry of Jesus including the calling of Peter and Andrew, James and John to leave their fishing nets to become 'fishers of men'.

After the feeding of so many, Jesus sent his disciples on ahead of him in the boat. They were to cross the Sea of Galilee in a northeasterly direction for a distance of some six miles to Bethsaida, just across the Galilean border. After the disciples started their journey Jesus then spent a little longer alone with the crowds and then he sent them away. I often wonder what Jesus might have said to the crowds when his disciples had left the scene – but I will never know the answer!

Jesus did not go around the Sea of Galilee to meet with his disciples in Bethsaida. Instead he climbed into the hills to be alone and to pray. If the tradition and speculation are correct, then Jesus went into the mountain-like cliffs of Arbel at the inland edge of the Plain of Gennesaret.

But the second part of Mark Chapter 6 continues with the boat full of disciples getting into difficulties in a sudden storm on the Sea. By this time it would have been very dark. If Mark's account is reasonably accurate then the boat, now somewhere in the middle of the Sea of Galilee, was way off course. Mark says that the disciples were rowing against the high wind that was hindering their progress towards Bethsaida. That surely meant that the wind was blowing from the north. The boat would have been too far to the south, tossed around by the winds and the raging sea.

This desperate rowing continued until almost the dawn. Then Jesus is said to have walked on the water to the boat, calming both the storm and the disciples. Notice that Mark's account of this incident goes on to imply that they never reached Bethsaida. Instead they returned to the Plain of Gennesaret where, over what must have been a period of many days, numerous people claimed to have been healed even by simply touching the cloak of Jesus [Mark 6:56].

It is important for us to read the mythos miracle stories in the context of their writing. They were written with the benefit of hindsight, in Mark's case looking back at least 30 years to the first Easter and reading the ancient Hebrew Scriptures into the community's experiences of Jesus of Nazareth. We need to put the individual miracle stories into the context of the Scriptures as a whole.

I am sure that when writing this, Mark was reminding Jews of their ancient story of God feeding Israel when Moses led them round and round in circles for 40 years after their escape from the Egyptian captivity. Mark was saying, "Remember how God took care of us all in the desert when we were hungry – now in our day of need as we live under the tyranny of Rome, Jesus is the one who similarly takes care of us. This is our experience and this is our story for today."

Mark duplicates Peter's stories

I often wonder why Mark included two stories of the feeding of thousands of people: 5000 in Chapter 6 and a further 4000 in Chapter 8? Are they the same story told twice, after all, they both take place in desert areas; they both have thousands present; they both have the same contents, loaves of bread and a few little fish?

Also, why did Mark include two stories of a storm-tossed boat and Jesus coming to the rescue, one in Chapter 4 and the other here in Chapter 6? Are they the same story told twice, and if so, why? Note that these two storm-tossed events concern only Jesus and his closest disciples – these storm stories are not part of the public ministry of Jesus. But what was the importance of the 'sea' within the Hebrew culture and tradition in which Mark was writing?

Marcus Borg, in his book *Jesus: A New Vision*, reminds us that the Hebrew Testament stories used the 'sea' as an image of chaos and evil that took them back to the Babylonian exile some 500-600 years before Jesus. Yet again the Jews had been defeated, conquered and exiled. In the attempt to assimilate the captives into their own culture, the Jews were exposed to the Babylonian Creation stories. One of them, the *Enuma Elish* was written 500 years or so before the Jews were exiled to Babylon. The Genesis Creation myths (and there are at least two versions in our Bible) are adaptations of the Babylonian *Enuma Elish* Creation myth written by the defeated Jews during the Babylonian exile.

What may be more surprising is that in the *Enuma Elish* the god of fertility, Apsu, is married to Tiamat, the primordial dragon and sea goddess. Apsu plans to murder two sons, a grandson and a great grandson, but before he can carry it out, Apsu himself is murdered. Tiamat is so incensed at the murder of her husband that she embarks on revenge and creates eleven monsters to help her. In this Babylonian Creation myth Tiamat, the evil sea goddess, symbolizes the forces of destruction, turmoil and chaos in the world.

But carefully note the following: the Hebrew word for the 'sea' or the 'deep' is *tehom* the equivalent word of the Babylonian *Tiamat.* The word *tehom* is there right at the beginning of the Book of Genesis Chapter 1 verse 2: "Now the earth was formless and empty, darkness was over the surface of the deep, and the Spirit of God was hovering over the waters." In Hebrew, "hovering over the *tehom.*"

In the Genesis Creation myth, the coded message to the captive Jews was simple: "Our God will overcome the chaos, turmoil and destructive power of the Babylonians! One day we will be free again!"

But there is more: the 'sea' continued to represent evil and God's overcoming power. It is there in the Book of Job in Chapter 38 verses 8 and 11, written just after the Babylonian exile: "Who shut up the sea behind doors when it burst forth from the womb… when I said, 'This far you may come and no farther; here is where your proud waves halt'?"

But there is yet more: the stories of Jesus stilling the storms were originally written more than 1000 years before the birth of Jesus. It is there in Psalm 107 verses 25 to 29:

> 25For he spoke and stirred up a tempest that lifted high the
> waves. 26They mounted up to the heavens and went down to
> the depths; in their peril their courage melted away. 27They
> reeled and staggered like drunkards; they were at their wits'
> end. 28Then they cried out to the LORD in their trouble, and
> he brought them out of their distress. 29He stilled the storm to
> a whisper; the waves of the sea were hushed.
> (New International Version)

Therefore, as I understand these issues, Mark's stories of these storms on the sea that were overcome by Jesus are telling of the godly power of Jesus to overcome not the sea itself but the evil represented by the ancient connotation of the 'sea'. Mark's coded message to his listeners and readers was, "Jesus never really walked on the water but the stories remind us that Jesus has fulfilled the Scriptures, right back to the beginning of the Genesis scroll."

Mark was also saying that what God had done in former times in taking care of the Hebrews and in overcoming the evil of foreign occupation and exile, the Jesus Spirit was also doing in the experiences of his followers by the same godly authority and power. In former times God had saved the people and Mark's account of the life of Jesus was that it was the Jesus Spirit that now could save the Jewish and gentile followers alike even within the evil of Roman Imperial oppression.

So was Mark telling history or was he telling a very powerful mythos story about something far greater? Was Mark supporting, encouraging and conveying, through story, the experiences of those who were following Jesus during the great persecution in Rome? In my understanding Mark's miracle stories of mass feeding and the stilling of storms at sea were wonderful mythos through which deep sacred truth was present. Sadly, because we Western Christians do not usually read the Scriptures with a Jewish mindset we miss the depth of Truth that is contained, not within the logos but within the mythos! We tend to literalize that which was 'security coded' within creative mythos text.

Personal experiences of the persecuted Christians

I have more questions: did Mark's story of Jesus get as far as Roman-occupied Israel during the disastrous Jewish rebellion?

Were Mark's stories the explanations of the persecuted as they trusted Jesus as the one who was strong to save and to get them through persecution and war?

Were these the stories of those who found comfort in their

experiences of the Jesus Spirit being greater than the forces of nature and the events and evils of life: exercising healing power over the 'raging winds and seas' and dispensing wisdom during the time of horrendous persecution in Rome and rebellion in Israel itself?

Jesus may have fed the thousands by some miracle or other. Jesus may have stilled the storms at sea, by one miracle or another. But I am convinced that these mythos stories were further examples of the social commentary of Peter/Mark. It was the personal experiences of the persecuted Christians that were of much greater importance to Mark and his community than the question of the historical accuracy of the coded mythos events described.

Similarly, in our increasingly secular age, it will be the truth of our experiences of the Jesus Spirit overcoming the chaos, turmoil and destructive powers that sometimes hit our personal lives that will be of much greater importance to us and to our skeptical family members, friends and colleagues than the question concerning the historical accuracy of the events described. It is in this questioning and in the interrogation of the Scriptures that I experience a far more vibrant and relevant Jesus than I ever knew when I was the kind of unquestioning Christian full of things that I believed because these were what preachers and leaders taught.

What is important to me now is rediscovering Jesus again and again for this world – the only world in which I can live. What I am concerned about is the extent to which I live in a way that is as true to my understanding of Jesus as I can get. It is not the way of logos literalism when I read the Scriptures, but, although not always successful, it is the way of seeking out the truth of the mythos and placing its compassion in the center of my day-to-day life. It is the way of accepting others as they are and not wanting them to become clones of me or of what I say. It really is the way of experiencing the Jesus Spirit constantly with me no matter what may be the chaos, the turmoil and the destructive powers that seem to be constantly unleashed all around us.

Need I remind us that every follower of the Jesus Way occupies a pulpit and preaches a constant sermon to everyone we meet, every day of our lives? Need I really remind us that the best way to preach the Good News of Jesus is not first by words, creeds or doctrines but by living compassionately and sacrificially thereby earning to right to use the words associated with our faith?

Mark Chapter 7:
Clean and unclean

We progress now into Mark 7:1-13 which tells of Pharisees and teachers of the Law travelling from Jerusalem to see for themselves just what Jesus was doing and saying.

Here we have Jesus being challenged by the Pharisees over the matter of what was considered to be clean or unclean. A sentence that speaks with so much relevance for me these days is Mark 7:8, "You have let go of the commands of God and are holding on to human traditions." [New International Version] There are two main questions that run throughout this section:

How can we understand the theology surrounding the life and death of Jesus unless we also know the historical contexts of the writings of the Jesus story?

Do we ever question how the Church in Britain, Canada, New Zealand, Australia, and increasingly even in the USA Bible Belt, has managed to get itself into its present sorry state?

There are ex-evangelicals like myself who have been accused of "letting go of the commands of God and of holding on to the traditions of men." But as Progressive Christians we attempt to do neither! What we do endeavor is to put living the compassionate and sacrificial lifestyle of Jesus before any purity of creed or doctrine.

But there is a major difficulty that both progressive and fundamentalist Christians have in common: there is little independent evidence to really know just what Jesus actually said and did. The nearest that we can get are hardly independent letters and Gospels – they are history remembered and history interpreted by those who were encouraging and supporting the development of their particular understanding of the Jesus Way. So I now ask a number of other important questions:

- When were the creeds and doctrines of the Christian Church developed?

• How many of the creeds and doctrines were introduced by Jesus himself?

• Are we any closer to the real words and actions of Jesus through the creeds, doctrines and traditions of the Church?

• Perhaps the most searching question of all is the one I repeat often in my preaching:

• To what extent would Jesus recognize himself and his teachings in the 3rd and 4th century creeds and doctrines that still dominate the Christian Church today?

The Gospel of Mark presents the first disciples of Jesus as tending to see him as a human being in whom they experienced something unique of God. Out of compassion Jesus accepted and affirmed those who were different: the social outcasts, the poor, and the hungry. Out of compassion he eventually treated women as his equal rather than as second-class possessions of either a father or a husband. He even taught his followers to deal compassionately with individual members of the Roman enemy. Indeed in the later Gospels of Matthew and Luke, written after the appalling Jewish rebellion against Rome and the destruction of the Jerusalem Temple, and as they were systematically being expelled from their synagogues, Jesus is retrospectively reputed to have said, "Love your enemies." [Matthew 5:44 and Luke 6:27 and 35]

In their experience of the ongoing presence of the Jesus Spirit, a life of compassion, sacrificial love and forgiveness was their Way of life together. But this was no soft option of quiet acquiescence. For example, in the story of paying taxes to Caesar, Jesus demonstrated that we are to respect the authority of those appointed to govern but he also gave us the example of challenging authority whenever it abused or exploited people.

The life of Jesus was not just a nice story with a gruesome ending, but a life of second chances and new beginnings: resurrection constantly offered to all. In my opinion, it is a life and example that should be ours today: we are those who are called to live the Jesus Way not just in theory and in Church, but in the way we sacrificially love and unconditionally accept difference; in the way in which we live compassionately and peaceably; in the way in which we nonviolently tackle any abusive political, religious or economic power. Although Jesus never spoke of himself as being part of the Trinity, and Trinity is not a Bible word, there is a contemporary trinity against which I attempt to make a stand.

The unholy trinity

It is the unholy trinity that exploits all of us and particularly undermines those who are in greatest need of social justice:

- The impact of globalization, unbridled banking systems and economic exploitation in which advertising runs roughshod over genuine needs and creates 'wants' so that their ceaseless greed constantly 'manufactures' market places for their goods and services.

- Military imperialism that says that 'might is right' and in which the most powerful nations attempt to impose their ideals and self-interests upon the poorer or less well-endowed military nations (oil and Iraq come readily to my mind).

- The subtle erosion of civil liberties in the name of national security. In Britain every single person who goes out of their home is caught on hundreds of CCTV cameras every single day. A friend from Lithuania once commented that not even under Stalin was he subjected to such surveillance and imposition by the authorities.

Progressive Christianity and social justice are inextricably joined. I love the Church and I need the Church, but Jesus Truth must come before the traditions that are so often those of men. If we can live the Jesus Way rather than to be overly concerned with traditions, creeds and doctrines; if we can avoid any statements that identify who is in and who is out; if our lives are based upon the experience of that which the Church has called 'Trinity' – the unity of compassion, equality, generosity of spirit, justice, peace, and perfect sacrificial love – then I am hopeful that there is a future for the Church and a better future for all humanity.

During or perhaps at the end of this encounter between Jesus and the Pharisees from Jerusalem, he again invited the crowd to gather around him. He commented immediately upon the accusations and hostile questioning of the Pharisees concerning the traditional rituals of hand washing, using certain cooking utensils and eating only those foods that customary Jewish teaching permitted. While the Pharisees were concerned with the corruption of both the body and the sacred by what people ate and swallowed, Jesus plainly taught that it was not what went into the body that corrupted it but it was the bowel waste, that "what comes out of a man that makes him 'unclean'."

I know that this 'bowel waste' is seen by many as unsavory when associated with Jesus and so commentaries often suggest that Jesus was really referencing the thoughts that emanate from the heart. May be, may be not, but the narrative does suggest that the reply of Jesus refers to both bowel waste and to the thoughts of the heart!

According to the narrative, at the end of this teaching session Jesus left the crowd and went back, probably, to his home in Capernaum. His disciples went with him and asked questions about what Jesus had just been teaching. Jesus seemed to be a little irritated by their questions, or perhaps he spoke with a broad smile on his face: "Are you so dull? Don't you see that nothing that enters a man from the outside can make him 'unclean'? Food goes to the stomach not to the heart!" [Mark 7:18-19]

What he next said would have continued his slide into further confrontation with the religious powers of the day because Jesus began commenting upon many contemporary social ills. He is reported to have said that the real problems facing people are not the result of eating unclean food but because we are all incomplete human beings living lives in which the following seem to arise all too readily: conceit, cruelty, defamation, dishonesty, foolishness, gluttony, immorality, infidelity, jealousy, malicious thoughts, murder, pilfering, sexual depravity and so on. All these evils are said, by Jesus, to come from inside and this is what makes us 'unclean' [Mark 7:20-23].

This really is the crux of this particular story: it was not by keeping laws, rules, regulations and traditions that made a man clean – indeed it was following such a lifestyle that made a man unclean. Cleanliness of heart was witnessed by living in ways that rejected this litany of human failure.

Jesus travels to gentile cities

After this return to his home in Capernaum, Mark next records Jesus setting off on his travels once again. Probably this time it was some 30 miles to the north of Capernaum on the important trade route to Hazor. From there it could have been another 25 miles in a straight line to the west. However, this was across rugged mountainous country and there is no evidence of any direct trade route or easy passage from Hazor into the region around the Phoenician coastal city of Tyre. Therefore, the obvious itinerary for Jesus and his disciples would have taken him on a minor trade route some 50 miles or so to the northwest from Hazor to Sidon, and then 25 or so miles back down the coast to Tyre.

Notice an important point from this geographical knowledge: Mark may not have known the geography of the area as he seems to suggest that Jesus visited Tyre before Sidon on this particular Jesus journey. Remember also that Mark had not been with Jesus but Peter had. Mark would have heard this story of Peter many times concerning his first major mission with Jesus into gentile country but it was quite conceivable that Mark took note of the names without understanding the geographical difficulties posed by a mountain range!

On the other hand, Mark simply records that Jesus went to the region around the city of Tyre but does not state categorically that Jesus went to Tyre itself. However, Mark does say that after the encounter with the Syro-Phoenician woman Jesus started his return journey via Sidon. Could this mean that Jesus visited Sidon twice, once on the outward and a second time on his return? But does it really matter? The important issues are why Jesus travelled to these gentile cities and what happened while he was in the region.

Both Sidon and Tyre were wealthy centers of commerce as part of a gentile area that was steeped in Canaanite paganism worshipping gods such as Baal and Ilu. Up to this point in the Peter / Mark version of the Jesus story, Jesus has more or less confined his wisdom teaching and healings to fellow Jews. So why, I wonder, did Jesus set his face to go to the pagan cities of Tyre and Sidon? Perhaps Sidon was important to Jesus in his uniting and reforming work because it had been the one major city that resisted Israel's conquering of Canaan at the time of Joshua? This was more than 1200 years before the life of Jesus. Was there something in the mind of Jesus that what Joshua had failed to do in military conquest Jesus intended to do with Yahweh's open love for all, Jew and gentile alike? [For more details concerning the importance of Baal to this story, see Appendix Nine.]

As I have said before, in my opinion Jesus was intent on both uniting and reforming the Judaism of his day, rather than having come to 'save' you and me. Was Jesus, whose life developed into breaking down the barriers that divided people, beginning to broaden his vision of Yahweh God's concern for all, Jew and gentile, male and female alike?

Was this the beginning of a new phase of ministry in which Jesus was attempting to redeem the past by [a] reconciling Jew and gentile, and [b] recognizing women as equal rather than as possessions of men? Had Jesus been successful in uniting Jew and Canaanite – that would have been some religious reformation! It would have heaped coals upon his head as far as the Pharisees and Sadducees were concerned. It may also have forged a strong but ultimately disastrous military alliance against Rome.

Did Jesus decide to leave Capernaum and other regions that were predominantly Jewish because his family and neighbors in Nazareth had recently rejected him? Or perhaps it was owing to the growing antagonism of his fellow Pharisees? Maybe he was now doing what he had earlier told his disciples to do following his rejection in Nazareth:

> 11 If any place will not welcome you or listen to you, leave that place and shake the dust off your feet as a testimony against them.
>
> [Mark 6:11 (New International Version)]

All this is speculation of course, but why else would Jesus the Jew have gone to the Canaanite gentile cities of Tyre and Sidon unless it was to meet with gentiles? It was here that the Syro-Phoenician woman, whom he called a 'dog', convinced him of the rightness of Yahweh's love for Jew and gentile alike [Mark 7:24-30]. This incident is, in my opinion, a story of prejudice and racism right at the heart of the Gospel.

Prejudice is always wrong. Racism is both evil and pernicious. From 1948 to 1994 the Dutch Reformed Church in South Africa upheld the evil racism of apartheid based upon its interpretation of the Hebrew Scriptures, modeling its theology on the Biblical nation of Israel.

Even in the USA the Bible was used and interpreted to justify racism until the early 1960s: the time of Martin Luther King; the bus boycotts; the freedom marches and black and white together proclaiming, "We shall overcome." It was not until 1964 that President Lyndon B. Johnson, signed the Civil Rights Act that ended legalized discrimination, but it seems to me that America still has to defeat Jim Crow for many within the poor black communities.

Racism is real and always destructive of people and whole communities. Even though Jesus was subject to being part of Pharisaic racism he began to change when he decided to travel into gentile country. However, it was being confronted by the faith of a gentile Syro-Phoenician woman that really sealed his new understanding and direction. From this point his entire discernment concerning both God and the Kingdom took on a whole new vision for Jesus. The wider that Jesus saw the grace and mercy of God then the more his authority grew and greater was his conflict with the Pharisees and the Sadducees. As his following grew so he was put increasingly onto a fatal collision course with both the Jewish religious leadership and the political leadership of the Roman Occupation Army.

Almost from the start of Mark's Gospel the Pharisees and teachers of the Law tried to undermine Jesus, including among his disciples. In Mark 2, Matthew 9 and again in Luke 5 the Pharisees went to the disciples while they and Jesus were eating with Matthew the tax collector and other men who were considered to be sinners. People usually find what they are looking for and here was Jesus, the one who not only healed but now forgave sins, ceasing to be holy in the eyes of the Pharisees: "How can a holy man eat with those whom we consider to be sinners?"

Only a fellow Pharisee would have been considered to be holy by other Pharisees! If Jesus had begun his ministry as a follower of the teaching of the Pharisees, or even as a Pharisaic Rabbi then he could no longer be one of them because their holiness was in keeping themselves apart from all that they considered to be 'unholy'. Jesus responded to them simply by saying, "I didn't come to invite good people [like you] to turn to God. I came to invite sinners." This was a direct attack upon the keystone of the Pharisaic way of life. Jesus was attacking the Pharisees by saying that God accepted those men whom the Pharisees rejected.

In sermons and Bible readings we hear so much about Pharisees, they receive a 'bad press' from the pulpits, but what do we know about them? Unless we have information how can we interpret the Christian Gospels accurately? For example, the Pharisees were not priests but they were a very important and powerful authority in the Law of Moses as seen within the written Hebrew Scriptures and told from their oral tradition.

They were the teachers and interpreters of the Law of Moses and, contrary to what we often are told, were especially well liked among the devout poor. Their painstaking path to holiness was by disengagement from those who did not follow their teaching, but it was a separation while living within the community. However, it was their conscientious adherence to the Law of Moses that made them into unyielding authoritarians. Their religiousness got in the way of their humanity. This is what the Parable of the Good Samaritan in Luke 10 is all about.

And there is another point in their favor. Whereas the Sadducees and their Temple Cult kept 'high' religion in the Jerusalem Temple, the Pharisees took religion to the synagogues in the towns and villages, making it more accessible to ordinary, albeit 'righteous' people. Jesus went one step further and reformed the religion of the synagogue, and then took it out to the ordinary people whom the Pharisees considered to be 'sinners'.

The turning point for Jesus

We consider again this gentile Syro-Phoenician woman. I interpret this as a probable logos story in which she changed the course of history. If it were not for her probably there would be no Christian Church today. Any followers of Jesus today probably would be in one of the Jewish sects that survived after the destruction of the Jerusalem Temple in 70 CE. Her importance must not be underestimated. Nor must we ignore the possibility that Jesus had commenced his ministry as a Pharisaic Rabbi. After all, he did keep himself apart from gentiles and even called this Syro-Phoenician woman in Mark 7 and Matthew 15 'a dog' – a belittling name of that time to describe gentiles.

I emphasize once again that, according to the Gospel of Mark, Jesus had already started his attempt to reform Pharisaic Judaism by mixing with fellow 'sinner' Jews and then gentiles whom the Pharisees considered to be unholy. (Note: nowhere in the Christian Testament can I find any evidence that Jesus had intended to start a Christian Church.) But this incident with the Syro-Phoenician woman was the key that unlocked his future ministry as he ceased to uphold [a] the old ways of Pharisaic holiness by racial and religious separation, and [b] the traditional social gender discrimination against women.

It was the turning point for Jesus in that he realized that God's love and compassion were for all – not just for the Pharisaic Jews and not just for the male of the human species. Jesus was moving on from the rules and regulations of the Pharisees to a new understanding and experience of God in which compassion and common sense were more important than the traditionalism of 'this is the way we have always done things around here' – one of the roots of institutionalized racism.

In my understanding of Mark's Gospel, until the incident with the Syro-Phoenician woman, all that Jesus had done in terms of healings and forgiving of sins had been directed at Jews alone. Even when Jesus travelled to the gentile city of Tyre the penny had not dropped for him concerning the place of women within Yahweh's universal love. He was blunt and particularly cruel towards her.

Her daughter had an evil spirit but the mother and daughter were not of the Jewish faith and therefore were beyond the care of Jesus. Now I have heard sermons from preachers who turned themselves inside out to explain that this was simply Jesus testing the faith of the woman. But I think these preachers have missed the point. Jesus was only concerned with Jews, and predominantly male Jews at that, because in the early Pharisaic understanding of Jesus, non-Jews were beyond the care of Yahweh God, and socially women were considered to be among the chattels of men.

When Jesus told her that she was like all gentiles, "a dog", the woman came back on this derogatory comment with her statement of faith that even the dogs eat the children's crumbs from under the table. To this gentile Syro-Phoenician woman Jesus replied, "For such a reply, you may go; the demon has left your daughter." [Mark 7:28-29]

In many respects this must have been a confirmation for Jesus that he has walked away from the Pharisaic teaching of holiness through separation from gentiles. From here on in Jesus really opened his heart, his mind and his ministry to see that God's love, compassion and mercy were for all people, not just for the Jews or for men alone. No wonder the separationist Pharisees wanted him dead!

Of all the women in the Hebrew and Christian Testaments my favorite has to be this gentile Syro-Phoenician woman. Without her persistence and act of faith Jesus probably would have continued his Pharisaic belief in holiness by racial and gender separation. Jesus had the courage to allow his thinking and life itself to be challenged and changed by the faith and actions of this gentile woman. That is, as always, a contemporary message beckoning both the Church and its members to adapt and to change to meet the demands of life in this our age.

Had Jesus not been confronted by this woman, doubtless the post-Easter followers of Jesus would have continued to be a small Jewish sect ministering to Jews alone. If this had happened then Saul of Tarsus, a Hellenistic Jew who was trying to marry Greek culture with traditional Judaism, probably would have had no reason to violently attack the early post-Easter followers of Jesus.

According to Philippians 3:5, Saul of Tarsus had been a Pharisee himself and therefore is it any wonder that this zealous young man wanted to protect his brand of Judaism from the breaking of the racial barriers that separated Jew and gentile? As we know, Saul of Tarsus went on to become the Apostle Paul, the self-appointed Apostle to the gentiles. As far as we can tell, it was Paul who first wrote about that 'something' that was very different in the lifestyle and loving ways of the Jews who followed Jesus. It happened in Antioch where Paul first coined the term 'Christian' to identify the Jewish and gentile converts who followed the Jesus Way from those fellow Jews who rejected the testimony and the experience of Jesus.

The Jesus ritual of healing

In returning to the story we find that Mark now has Jesus leaving the region around Tyre and, rather than immediately going south into Jewish territory, has him travelling north back to Sidon, deep into gentile territory. From there Jesus seems to have retraced his steps back towards Hazor but before reaching Jewish Capernaum Jesus went around the top of the Sea of Galilee into another gentile region, that of Decapolis [Mark 7:31-37].

When the people there realized whom it was who was returning to this region, and remembering the healing of the madman of Gerasa [Mark 5:1-20], they came out to meet Jesus once again. Some even brought a deaf man to him. They pleaded with Jesus to heal him. Jesus led him away from the crowd and then did something very strange. He put his fingers into the man's ears and then, after removing the fingers, spat onto his own hands.

What then followed was hardly a hygienic healing process: earwax and spittle placed onto the man's tongue. But as Jesus did this, Mark has him looking up to the sky and saying, "Ephphatha!" which means, 'be opened!'. Instantly the ears were unblocked and the man began to talk normally. Although Jesus then commanded the man to keep quiet about this healing neither he nor the people who were looking from a distance could keep silent. They had seen all the good things that Jesus had done, including enabling the deaf to hear and the silent to speak [Mark 7:37].

This passage again raises a number of issues for me concerning the healing process and the significance of making the deaf hear and the silent to speak. It seems to me that Jesus had developed a ritual of healing, although it was not always used:

- Out of compassion Jesus took the initiative and often, but not always, led the person concerned away from the crowds.

- Jesus then touched the person concerned at the place where the healing was sought (i.e. ears; tongue; eyes; etc).

- This touch certainly got the attention of the person concerned.

- Jesus announced that the healing had been accomplished, not because of what he himself had done but because the person concerned had faith.

This can be seen in Mark 1:40-42, Matthew 8:2-4 and Luke 5:12-14 with the healing of the man who was suffering from leprosy; Mark 7:32-34 with the healing of the deaf man who, not surprisingly, also had speech problems; Mark 8:21-23 with the healing of a blind man at Bethsaida; Matthew 20:29-34 with two blind men receiving their sight as Jesus and his disciples were leaving Jericho.

There is also the incident of the woman who touched the hem of the cloak of Jesus and was healed [Mark 5:25-34]. Jesus again said that this was the result of the woman's faith. Furthermore, there is another incident of touching and healing where the faith of the person concerned was not involved: Luke 22:50-52 has Jesus at the moment of his arrest healing the ear of the servant of the high priest.

So, here with the healing of this deaf and speech-impaired man [Mark 7:31-37] we once again see the healing ritual. Surely Jesus could not fail to get the attention of the man when he stuck a finger in each ear! And having got the attention of the man Jesus then spat on his own hands and spread the spittle onto the tongue of the deaf man. What medical use was either of these actions? None at all, but psychologically the man was totally hooked like a fish on the line. Such unusual actions certainly raised the expectation of the man so that the level of faith was raised to such intensity self-healing took place.

I have no doubt that some miraculous occurrences did take place when Jesus performed his healing rituals. However, there is just one question that still hangs at the back of my mind about Mark's story: "Was this Peter / Mark record of the healing of deaf and blind people mythos, logos or Midrash?"

This I ask because there is an important link between the coming of the Kingdom and a prophecy of 1st Isaiah Chapter 29. The prophet is attacking the behavior of God's people who are descended from King David. He accuses them of paying lip service to the rules and Laws of God:

> 13The Lord says: "These people come near to me with their mouth and honor me with their lips, but their hearts are far from me. Their worship of me is based on merely human rules they have been taught." [Isaiah 29:13 (New International Version)]

Was this not an accurate description of the Pharisees and Sadducees at the time of Jesus? But there is more: Isaiah 29:17 says, 17In a very short time, will not Lebanon be turned into a fertile field and the fertile field seem like a forest? (New International Version) Please do not miss the significance of the reference to Lebanon – Tyre and Sidon, those gentile pagan cities were and remain part of what we still call Lebanon!

Was Jesus taking upon himself this prophecy of 1st Isaiah to go to them and, in so doing, was he taking the blessing that the Jews believed had been intended for them alone and offering it to the gentiles of Lebanon? Was Jesus acting out the ancient prophecy that had been written some eight centuries before? After all, Jesus knew his Torah and the scrolls of the prophets. Recently he also had been rejected by his fellow Jews in Nazareth and was increasingly criticized by the Jewish religious establishment back in Judea and Galilee. Perhaps his visit to Tyre and Sidon may have been a temporary symbolic kicking of the traditional Jewish dust from off his feet? But still we are not at the end of what 1st Isaiah had to say: 18 In that day the deaf will hear the words of the scroll, and out of gloom and darkness the eyes of the blind will see. [Isaiah 29:18 (New International Version)]

Mark now confirms Peter's interpretation of the rightness of Jesus going to the gentiles in Lebanon, taking God's blessing from the Jews and offering it to the gentiles, in this one of the many mythos healing stories: "Now that we have been to Lebanon, Jews and gentiles alike now know that the time of God's great blessing has come because the deaf hear and the blind see!"

So, did the healings of the man who was suffering from leprosy, or the deaf man who also had speech problems, or a blind man at Bethsaida, or two blind men at Jericho really happen? Were they logos history retold or mythos stories packed with sacred truth concerning the coming of the new age prophesied by 1st Isaiah and embodied in Jesus of Nazareth? Or maybe they were Midrash stories, taking the ancient tales and retelling them in the present to demonstrate that in Jesus the 1st Isaiah 29 prophecy had been fulfilled! But these are the wrong questions because it does not matter whether or not these stories really happened. Once again I say that the importance of these stories is what they might mean for us today.

Mark Chapter 8:
Do you still not understand?

I assume, rightly or wrongly, that the feeding of the 5000 in Mark 6 is actually the same mythos story retold at the beginning of Mark 8:1-10. Here Jesus is reported to have fed another 4000 men, this time with seven loaves and a few small fish. After everybody was fed there were seven large baskets of leftovers collected.

According to the narrative, after feeding the 4000 Jesus and his disciples crossed the lake once more. They beached in the Jewish territory near Dalmanutha, just north of the gentile spa town of Tiberias. The Pharisees came to meet Jesus and started an argument with him, demanding a sign from heaven to confirm his ministry [Mark 8:11-13].

Jesus, somewhat in exasperation, told them he would give them no such sign. It was as though the Pharisaic challenge was further confirmation for Jesus that his ministry at that time was probably better among the gentiles than the Jews. And with that, Jesus and the disciples got back into the boat and crossed over once again to the gentile eastern side of the Sea.

The disciples then realized that they had no bread with them, apart from one loaf. Jesus took this situation and turned it into a teaching opportunity [Mark 8:14-21]. Here Jesus warned them to be careful of the "yeast of the Pharisees and that of Herod." But the disciples were unable to understand what Jesus was saying. They assumed that Jesus was criticizing them for having insufficient bread: just the one loaf.

Jesus then asked them, "Why are you talking about having no bread? Do you still not see or understand? Are your hearts hardened? Do you have eyes but fail to see, and ears but fail to hear? And don't you remember? When I broke the five loaves for the five thousand, how many basketfuls of pieces did you pick up?"

The disciples answered, "Twelve."

But Jesus continued and asked yet another puzzling question, "When I broke the seven loaves for the four thousand, how many basketfuls of pieces did you pick up?"

The disciples answered, "Seven."

Jesus challenged them, "Do you still not understand?"

The disciples did not understand – and I am really none the wiser! I can only guess at an answer that satisfies my curiosity at this time. This is a direct reference again back to 1st Isaiah. Here was Jesus still having problems with his own disciples and their ability to discern what Jesus was saying and doing: "you have eyes but fail to see, and ears but fail to hear?"

Perhaps all Jesus was saying, and told to us through the memories of Peter was, "Pay attention to what you have seen and heard! Do not pay too much attention to the accusations and arguments of the religious Pharisees and political Herodians – those who are on the side of the King. Just like yeast is used in cooking bread to change the dough, if you pay too much attention to the religious and political Establishment the 'yeast' of their words will change our ministry and our message – and not for the better!"

Whatever the meaning of that section of Mark's Gospel might be, we come now to a gap in the chronology of the story. An unknown amount of time has passed and we next find Jesus and his disciples having returned once more to the northeastern shore of the Sea of Galilee. They were entering Bethsaida [Mark 8:22-26]. As mentioned a couple of pages ago, here is another example of the healing ritual of Jesus:

- Jesus led the blind man away from the crowds.

- Jesus then spat into and touched the blind eyes.

- This touch ensured the whole attention of the blind man.

This time Jesus had to repeat part of the healing ritual so that the partially restored sight was completely restored. Notice, however, in Peter's recall, on this occasion Jesus did not speak of faith at all.

Perhaps it was the compassion of Jesus that successfully increased the expectation of the blind man? Perhaps this, coupled with the remarkable ability of mind over matter, was what gave sight to the blind man?

But, no matter how this happened or what was the source of the healing, in the narrative an inexplicable event had taken place. Mythos or logos? Once again, each reader must come to their own conclusion on such matters. The important point is this: we should live out what these stories say to each one of us today as we follow the Jesus Way.

Mark once more has Jesus and his disciples moving north from Bethsaida to the villages around the gentile city of Caesarea Philippi [Mark 8:27-30]. As they were walking along Jesus entered into conversation with them and asked what they thought that others were saying about him. The answers were specific: "John the Baptist, Elijah or one of the other great prophets from our history." But then Jesus put them on the spot and went to the heart of the challenge, "But who do you say that I am?"

This question attributed to Jesus has caused many controversies that have split church after church since the end of the first century – just who was and how human was Jesus? Those who followed Jesus in the early years thought of him as an ordinary human being who had developed immense God qualities and in whom they knew that they had met the divine presence. He then became thought of as 'Lord' and his divinity began to overtake the discussions. There followed immense controversy among the different communities of Christians as to the extent to which Jesus was human or God, or a balance between the two. Justin Martyr [100-165 CE] argued that Jesus was to the Father as the rays of light are to the sun, subordinating Jesus to the Father. Then along came Irenaeus [130-200 CE] with the theology that Jesus, as the Son of Man, humbled himself to become like us so that we could become like him [God]. Irenaeus was a theological forerunner in that he experienced God as an emerging Trinity. Origen [185-254

CE] then entered the arguments by saying that God was only Father and Son, both being of the same substance but that the Father was the more important of the two. Tertullian [160-225 CE] developed the theology of Irenaeus into the full-blown Trinity that we know today. And so it went on until Constantine 'converted' to Christianity in an attempt to seal the Empire with one orthodox Christian religion – hence the 4th century Councils that gave us the Creeds.

"But who do you say that I am?"

So this question of Jesus "But who do you say that I am?" was both for then and for today. We each make our decision on the matter that will suffice us for the time being. Where I am now I see Jesus as Spong explains, no different to us in substance (i.e. he was human) but very different in degree (i.e. reflecting the fullness of humanity where I am convinced we also can experience divinity). So Jesus was the same flesh and blood human as we are, but his life was lived in such fullness of humanity that people either said he was God or he was the devil in disguise to lead people astray. So I see Jesus as not being less human than us, but more human! The joy of this is that if Jesus, a human, could attain such divine qualities, then so can we. But Peter's immediate response to this "Who is Jesus?" question was, "You are the Messiah!" Jesus then warned the disciples not to tell anyone about this or what they thought of him. However, was this really Peter's response at the time that Jesus supposedly asked the question, or is this a theological insight based upon Peter's retrospective interpretation and growing knowledge of whom he thought Jesus had been?

What then follows seems to interrupt the flow of the story. Having had the deep revelation that Jesus was the Messiah and all the personal greatness and power that would come with that in freeing the people from foreign domination, Peter could not contain himself. He told Jesus to stop talking about predicting his own death. The response of Jesus was, "Get behind me, Satan! You do not have in mind the things of God, but the things of men."

Mark Chapter 9:
Discipleship will be costly

In one sense the last section of the previous chapter [Mark 8:31-Mark 9:1] separates the recognition by Peter of the Messiahship of Jesus and the event six days later that we call the Transfiguration of Jesus [Mark 9:2-13]. However, on close inspection the apparent barrier between these two passages is not an obstacle at all! This intervening passage has Peter / Mark mapping out what was going to happen to Jesus at the hands of the religious and political establishments. Peter seems to recall that it was important that the followers of Jesus were given a clear understanding of what they were getting themselves into. But again, was this an actual conversation between Peter and Jesus or was it Peter's recall based within his developing theological understanding of Jesus?

No matter how one looks at it, this 'Satan' statement was a terrible rebuke. Peter was associated with the Enemy rather than with God. Peter and the disciples, like the crowds that followed Jesus wherever he went, were still expecting an earthly king to rid the nation of the Romans. Then in the developing story Peter / Mark included the calling of the crowds and the disciples together and Jesus pronouncing that if anyone wanted to follow him there must be self-denial to the extent of taking up a personal cross. Jesus added that anyone who wanted to continue living his own life would actually lose it, but whoever gave up his/her own life to follow Jesus and to live for the Gospel would find a new fulfilling life!

I am not convinced that Jesus said such a thing openly to the crowd, especially as he was trying to stop this talk of Messiah getting out of hand. In my thinking, here is Peter recalling an incident in which he himself is highly criticized by Jesus and yet he is happy for the story to be told at cost to himself. This is Peter looking lovingly at the Jesus followers in Rome during the time of persecution and perhaps seeing some of the faithful wavering and thinking of giving it all up, and of others hanging on in spite of executions by fire, gladiator or lion.

Here is Peter explaining the importance of the cross and the execution of Jesus. The death of Jesus was, at the time of his execution, devastating for his followers who simply could not make sense of their hope for the future hanging dead on the cross. Now, some three decades on, Peter sees the victory of the cross in both the joy and the cost of discipleship.

Also Peter is saying, "Look, I got it wrong! I wanted Jesus to be our great leader in rebellion against Rome. I even attempted to defend Jesus with the sword at the moment of his arrest! But I stayed with Jesus even beyond his death. Now I ask you to stay with Jesus. What good is it for a man to gain the whole world, yet forfeit his soul? Or what can a man give in exchange for his soul? If anyone is ashamed of Jesus and his words in this adulterous and sinful generation, the Son of Man will be ashamed of him when he comes in his Father's glory with the holy angels."

Whether or not Jesus actually said these words really does not matter. Even if they were only creative words of encouragement to the followers of the Jesus Way living through that time of bloody persecution in Rome and ascribed to Jesus by Peter, it is immaterial. The important issue is that within the mythos or the logos, Peter/Mark discovered that the Namaste Spirit remained faithful, close and within the followers of Jesus, no matter what the cost to each one may be.

Jesus, Moses, Elijah and John the Baptist

As the Peter/Mark story of Jesus unfolds we are now presented with the second half of the 'Who is Jesus?' episode. We read [Mark 9:2-13] that Jesus took three disciples with him to the top of a mountain. In all probability this would have been Mount Hermon whose summit is in present-day Syria on the border with Lebanon and the Israeli-controlled Golan Heights. The nearest town at the time of Jesus would have been Caesarea Philippi.

Here, in the story of the Transfiguration of Jesus, we have a fuller explanation of the links between Jesus and Moses, Elijah and John the Baptist. I have written in much greater detail of the Transfiguration of Jesus in *Setting Jesus Free* [pages 68-75] so all that I will add at this moment is that the Peter/Mark retrospective account explicitly links, yet again, Jesus with the fulfillment of the ancient Scriptures concerning Elijah and the Messiah. The ancient Hebrew thinking was that Elijah must come again before the great and awful day of the Lord. But there was no obvious evidence, at least to the disciples, that Elijah had returned. In answer to this puzzlement for them Jesus said:

> 13But I tell you, Elijah has come, and they have done to him everything they wished, just as it is written about him.
> [Mark 9:13 (New International Version)]

When? Where? Who? Have you noticed that the missing person from the second half of the 'Who is Jesus/the Transfiguration' stories is John the Baptist? Here, using the gift of historical hindsight and theological interpretation, Peter/Mark are attributing to Jesus the explicit link between Elijah and the Baptist! In other words, for Peter/Mark, Elijah has come again in the form of John the Baptist. Consequently Jesus of Nazareth now can be considered as the Christ/the Messiah. This probably is a literary device – an interpretative explanation rather than an accurate historical record of what Jesus may or may not have said.

According to the narrative Jesus, accompanied by his three disciples, then journeyed back down to the plain where a crowd had gathered [Mark 9:14-29]. As they approached they became aware of an argument going on between the other disciples and the teachers of the Law of Moses. I suspect that these learned men were rebuking and mocking the other disciples because a father had brought his son to Jesus for healing. Not finding Jesus the father had implored the remaining disciples to force the demon out of his son. Although they tried, the disciples failed to chase out the demon. Bearing in mind that they had previously experienced successful healings and exorcisms [Mark 6:6-13] perhaps they had become too blasé about the rituals taught them by Jesus?

Then again, reading verse 18 carefully one can identify the symptoms, not of demon possession but of what we now call a grand mal seizure. The son was probably suffering regular epileptic attacks but the father, acting within the scope of medical science of the day, attributed the illness to demon possession. The disciples had failed hence the rebuke and the mocking on the part of the teachers of the Law of Moses.

When Jesus enquired and was told what had been happening, his immediate response was again one of exasperation: You unbelieving people, how long will I be able to stay with you? Even more importantly, how long will I be able to put up with you? "Bring the boy to me."

This could have been a criticism of a number of people. It could have been an attack upon the teachers of the Law of Moses. It could equally have been a criticism of the ordinary people in the crowd, possibly both Jew and gentile. Or most likely it was an accusation once again against his own disciples. After all, just a week or so before Jesus seemed to have been highly critical of their looking at but not seeing the truth of what he was doing – the incident in the boat when there was but one loaf of bread [Mark 8:21]. He was also critical again of some of the disciples, especially Peter, who had been thinking that Jesus was to be the political Messiah who would lead them in victory against Rome.

It is comforting for many people today to understand him as 'gentle Jesus, meek and mild'. However, we need also to recognize that Jesus was capable of getting angry but his anger had been reserved for the Pharisees and Sadducees. Nevertheless in getting close to Peter's story of his experiences of Jesus I begin to see, not so much the man from Nazareth as being too divine to be of earthly use, but as a man whose compassion and love was paramount. Here was Jesus, a man whose compassion got him really angry and exasperated even with those who were close to him. Here was a real man of the earth, part of living in the dirt and gutters of life.

Confronting wrongdoing and evil

It is easy also to allow ourselves to be blinded by what we think was the compassion of Jesus so that we are so loving and kind that we upset nobody. Having read *Setting Jesus Free* Brian Wilson wrote to me in response to my references to living 'the Jesus Way'. He stated that there was, on my part, "a degree of oversimplification when relating Jesus' teaching to modern contexts – e.g. page 131 on the IRA. Does the bully or fanatic ever listen to reason that isn't backed by strength? Is there no morality? … How are we to confront wrongdoing – and even more, evildoing?"

Earlier in this book I quoted Kipling. Brian Wilson did something similar for me, by adding a couple of his own verses to Kipling's poem *The Gods of the Copybook Heading*:

> Then came the post-modern era, and the churches came tumbling down;
> Progressives cried, "We have the answer," and welcomed all-comers to town.
> "The hope of the future's INCLUSION; nothing else mattered; anything goes."
> They cried, "Feed the feckless and foolish; Agape love for our foes."
> But the Gods of the Copybook Headings simply smiled, and then waited, until
> The progressives had spoken and lectured – and let others pick up the bill.
> Fundamentalists preached Armageddon; the Islamists cried for Jihad.
> And the plain, simple, ordinary man in the street just made do with what little he had.

That came as a salutary reminder to me that the compassion of Jesus was not and cannot be that of 'anything goes'. My answer to Brian's humorous but nonetheless forthright and challenging statement must surely be in offering a different perception concerning Jesus. Perhaps we need to present him and his compassion today, not as a 'goodie two shoes' who smiles at everyone, but as a man who would be at home among the winos of London or the Crips and Bloods, Florencia 13 and 18th Street gangs of Los Angeles?

Although I am sure that he would not be wielding a gun or knife, perhaps he would be just as at home at the Joint Base Andrews Naval Air Facility Washington or on board the Type 23 frigate HMS St. Albans or with the Marine Corp or the SAS in Iraq or Afghanistan. But probably he would be on the front line in Palestine with the Quaker Peace and Social Witness Ecumenical Accompaniment Program. Compassion does not mean lying down, rolling over and letting everyone walk over the poor or even over ourselves. In the context of the sacred, 'compassion' is not a noun but a very active verb.

In the story of the healing of the epileptic boy Jesus touched his hand (the ritual again) and helped him to stand after yet another grand mal attack. Then, in answer to the disciples' question, "Why couldn't we drive it out?" Jesus replied, "This kind can come out only by prayer." [Mark 9:28-29] In Peter's understanding it was the power of prayer, additional to the belief of the father that had been encouraged by Jesus, that healed the boy. Today, although it is not a cure, the treatment would be by medication such as Felbatol, Gabitril and Lyrica.

An additional point to ponder concerning this story of the healing of the epileptic boy is the use of two Greek verbs *egeiren* and *aneste* in verse 27: "But Jesus took him by the hand and lifted him to his feet, and he stood up." [NIV] But translated differently and perhaps more accurately as "But Jesus took him by the hand, and raised him up; and he arose." [American Standard Version] Perhaps Peter was creating a literary prelude to the passage that follows immediately after the healing of the boy?

> [30]They left that place and passed through Galilee. Jesus did not want anyone to know where they were, [31]because he was teaching his disciples. He said to them, "The Son of Man is going to be delivered into the hands of men. They will kill him, and after three days he will rise." [32] But they did not understand what he meant and were afraid to ask him about it. [Mark 9:30-32 (New International Version)]

In the development of this carefully crafted story, Peter/Mark may have been using *egeiren* and *aneste,* because they are both technical terms associated with resurrection. Maybe there was a logos incident in which Jesus cured an epileptic boy and upon which Peter/Mark constructed a mythos? Or maybe it was just a wonderful creative story – a *mythistoricus* as part of the developing 'narrative' or a 'myth-novel' that we call Mark's Gospel? But I remind you yet again, even a *mythistoricus* is packed with sacred truth.

Jesus and his disciples returned once again to his home in Capernaum [Mark 9:33-37]. Along the way the disciples were arguing among themselves and when they were 'back at home' Jesus asked them, "What were you arguing about on the road?"

Not surprisingly they kept quiet because they were arguing among themselves as to who was the most important disciple as far as Jesus was concerned. Was it John or Peter, or even Mary Magdalene? Jesus must have had a suspicion as to the nature of the debate, even if he had not exactly overheard the conversation itself. He gathered the twelve principal disciples and said, "If anyone wants to be first, he must be the very last, and the servant of all."

There is no doubt in my mind that a crowd had gathered again around the home of Jesus because somewhere nearby was at least one child. Jesus took the child into his arms and said to the disciples, "Whoever welcomes one of these little children in my name welcomes me; and whoever welcomes me does not welcome me but the one who sent me."

Being first, last, servant and a small child

This is a strange episode in Mark's Gospel. What has being first and last and the servant of all in the Kingdom have to do with welcoming a small child? Also, why does the story jump around between servant-hood, possessive pride and millstones around the neck? How many sermons have I both heard and preached that have taken the line that entrance into God's Kingdom is by setting aside all knowledge, status, power and so on and coming to Jesus as a small child would come: trusting and receptive to him and to his message?

As I see things now such self-denial denigrates the individual concerned and denies the possibility of 'humanity's fullness' within all people. We should come into the experience of the Kingdom not by belittling ourselves but by rejoicing in the sacred presence within us, along with gifts and personal skills that we have, so that they can be given away as an offering that will develop both ourselves and others.

Having said that, I do interpret this incident with the child as a statement that reflected the lack of importance of children at that time. They were without legal status other than being the possession of the father and physically powerless to change anything of importance that impacted upon them. Jesus was pointing out to those of his disciples who continued to see the Kingdom in terms of the social, political and religious hierarchies of importance that existed in their world that the Kingdom was not made up of such things. Just as women of his day were low status possessions so children had a similar low status. Jesus was pointing out that in the Kingdom of God the love of power to control (male) was to be rejected but the power of love and servant-hood (female and children) was to be the praxis of life.

Although this quick succession of stories might seem to be disjointed they were, in fact, important and linked teaching points. They were also presented as a literary device to enable Peter/Mark to demonstrate that the disciples really were slow to understand the nature and the purpose of the work of the Kingdom. This becomes evident once again in Mark 10:35-45 where the disciples still were none the wiser. We will explore that part of the story of servant-hood greatness a little later.

The Peter/Mark narrative now moves to a debate as to who is for or against the work of Jesus [Mark 9:38-41]. John was puzzled because the disciples had seen a man driving out demons in the name of Jesus but he and his companions had commanded him to stop, "because he was not one of us." How often, I wonder, has the servant-hood work of the Kingdom been stunted by possessive pride of clergy and laity concerning their assigned roles and responsibilities?

"We are the chosen! We are the ones to do this work. We have turned around our collars. It is ours. Don't get involved unless you are one of us!" Possessive pride kills and Jesus is recorded to have replied:

> 39"Do not stop him," Jesus said. "For no one who does a miracle in my name can in the next moment say anything bad about me, 40for whoever is not against us is for us. 41Truly I tell you, anyone who gives you a cup of water in my name because you belong to the Messiah will certainly not lose their reward.
> [Mark 9:39-41 (New International Version)]

There is much that can be said about those who are for or against Jesus. Indeed, the Gospel texts are contradictory on this issue. Luke 9:49-50 takes the Peter/Mark narrative and repeats it word for word. However, Matthew 12:30 has the exact opposite: "He who is not with me is against me, and he who does not gather with me scatters." I will say no more at this point other than that I have explored this in much greater detail in *Setting Jesus Free* [pages 75-81] linking these sayings right back to the Hebrew Testament stories of Micah, 1st Isaiah and Joel.

Creating a stumbling block

What follows is another strange passage that seems to me to be out of place [Mark 9:42-50]. It is concerned with the behavior of anyone who thus creates a stumbling block before one of these children. (But are these 'children' in age, or in faith, or in attempting to follow the Jesus Way: this is an ongoing scholarly debate!) But no matter how serious it may have been to cause another to sin, this passage was never intended to be subjected to a literal interpretation. Surely, no one was then, or is now, expected to cut off hands or feet or to pluck out eyes because these either have been used in sinful actions or may be used to lead one into sin. These, along with the millstone tied around the neck before the sinner is thrown into the sea and drowned, are expressions of the gravity of leading another into sin. None of these were intended by Jesus or Peter/Mark to be either a self-inflicted or a legal system punishment for sins committed. A similar debate continues to this day concerning the purpose, relevance and severity of the penal codes in nation after nation. Is justice best served by 'lock them up and throw away the key' or by something different, such as restorative justice when appropriate to the crime?

This passage also contains references to an eternal casting 'into hell' or to 'be thrown into hell' but these were descriptions arising from the worldview of the time. They are irrelevant and inappropriate to our world today. As far as I am concerned there is enough of both heaven and hell on earth to satisfy and to challenge me in the here and now. If there is heaven or hell beyond this life I am sure that whatever 'God' is can worry about that. My concern is living the Kingdom now. If there is life or eternal fire beyond death then it is not 'somewhere out there' but in the people, the impact and the legacy that we leave behind for future generations.

I am certainly disinterested in living this life as a preparation for the next. We pass this way once and have moment-by-moment choices as to the extent to which we live the Jesus Kingdom Way. Death is a natural part of life. It is something that we usually try to put off for as long as possible but life is to be lived now, sacrificially, abundantly (but not possession based), unconditionally – that's the Perfect Love that I experience and understand to be the Jesus Way. That's good enough for me.

There is yet another strange and seemingly out of place statement at the end of this passage: "Salt is good, but if it loses its saltiness, how can you make it salty again? Have salt among yourselves, and be at peace with each other." [Mark 9:50 (New International Version)]

This is not a statement about cooking but about action. Salt is good for sterilizing and protecting against a variety of unpleasant and harmful bacteria. It adds flavor to food. It is also a fertilizer but used in the wrong place can ravage the environment. Peter/ Mark talked of 'salt' as a way of life: cleansing, flavoring and encouraging growth. If we could all live in such humane ways then we would all be at peace with each other!

Before leaving this passage there is one further comment to be made. Increasingly biblical scholars are discussing whether or not Jesus actually said any of these words attributed to him concerning hands, feet, eyes or millstones. Even if he did, were all of these in one teaching 'slot' with his disciples? Perhaps these were spoken of in different places, at different times and in different contexts? Perhaps Jesus even repeated these many times over, but they were brought together as a single strand of teaching by the author of the Gospel narrative. It is the prerogative of an author to create a story out of disjointed and displaced events. To rearrange the pieces of the logos to create a mythos story is not the same as misleading or misrepresenting either the person or the incidents.

Mark Chapter 10:
Concerning family life

Notice that we are now well into a section of Mark's Gospel concerning family life that began at Mark 9:36 with a child, and continues to Mark 10:16 with the blessing of children. Between these two 'bookends' there is some difficult teaching on the subject of divorce [Mark 10:1-12].

According to the narrative Jesus and his disciples started out again from Capernaum. This time it was south into Judea, a Roman Province and then across the Jordan probably into Perea, possibly south of Jericho and over to somewhere in the vicinity of Bethany Beyond the Jordan. This is significant because Galilee and Perea, although separated geographically by Samaria, were part of the kingdom that had been allocated by the Roman occupiers to Herod Antipas. This was the king who had imprisoned and then executed John the Baptist a short while before, particularly because John the Baptist had publicly criticized the marriage of King Herod Antipas to Herodias, the wife of his brother Philip.

Jesus was not escaping Herod Antipas, nor was he going to teach and heal the gentiles because Perea was still predominantly Jewish. Therefore the teaching on divorce had two major targets: his Jewish compatriots in general and King Herod Antipas in particular.

Jesus refers to the teaching of Moses that reinforced the situation then (and even today among some Jews) that the man could divorce the wife almost at the drop of a hat, but the wife had no right to divorce her husband. Why not? Because once again we see that the wife was the property of the husband to be used almost at his whim and fancy.

In this story there were some Pharisees who went to Jesus to test him on his knowledge of the Law of Moses. They were the experts and they went with this question about the lawfulness of a man divorcing his wife to test Jesus. Again we see the wisdom of Jesus who turned the question back on the questioner. "What did Moses command you?" he replied.

The Pharisees, perhaps somewhat taken aback, went on the offensive: "Moses permitted a man to write a certificate of divorce and send her away."

Whereas the Pharisees saw nothing wrong in a man disposing of his belongings in such a way, Jesus opened up a whole new line of accusation based upon compassion for the divorced woman. "It was because your hearts were hard that Moses wrote you this law but at the beginning of creation God made them male and female."

This statement is repeated in wedding liturgy all the time: God made them male and female. Jesus did not support the ancient understanding that God first made man and then the woman as his subordinate. Instead, according to the Gospel record, Jesus emphasized that, upon marriage, a man leaves his father and mother not to be the possessor of a wife but to be united as one flesh.

This was radical teaching for Jewish men at that time. Marriage was not to be a matter of property and possessions but of equality between man and wife. Jesus said, "So they are no longer two, but one."

I know that I can be accused of reading into this story that which may not have been the case. But it seems to me that this interpretation fits well with the ways in which the Gospels record Jesus dealing with women. He disregarded the taboos of the time. He talked openly with unaccompanied women, even those who were not Jewish by birth. He defended the woman taken in adultery when the Law of Moses commanded stoning to death.

Decisions about divorce

Jesus did not uphold the belief that God had favored the men when it came to decisions about divorce. However, many parts of the Christian Church today still practice the very letter rather than the spirit of the Law that Jesus seemed to introduce: "Therefore what God has joined together, let man not separate."

Divorce is not something that one enters into lightly. But for the Church to condemn divorce outright seems to me to be following the letter rather than the spirit of such a law: legalism rather than compassion. I fully accept the wonder and sanctity of marriage but sometimes marriages just do not work. Where is the compassion in the public pretense that a marriage is fine or insisting that there is no divorce possible while the lives of the husband and wife, and worse still the lives of any children, are private battlefields, destructive of all involved? Jesus said that marriage was a God-thing – it was sacred and perhaps he did add, "let man not separate."

This "let man not separate" has been interpreted for centuries as "the church has joined these two together in matrimony, so do not let the laws of the State separate them." It may mean just that, but I think that when we put this incident back into its context of the compassion and radicalism of Jesus, then it really did mean (and still does mean) exactly as it says: "let no *man* separate." Perhaps this was Jesus, according to the Peter / Mark record saying, "Women have just as many rights in the Kingdom of God as men. Divorce should be the last resort but if it becomes necessary then it should be equally available to the woman as it is, by the male interpretation of the Law of Moses, available to the man."

This for Jesus, "let man not separate" is not so much a case of legalism but a matter of gender equality. However, even when a further seemingly harsh comment is attributed to Jesus concerning divorce, I am convinced that it was to show the severity of the impact of such an action rather than to make divorce illegal: "Anyone who divorces his wife and marries another woman commits adultery against her. And if she divorces her husband and marries another man, she commits adultery."

Church denominations continue to proclaim that marriage is both sacred and for life, but many also recognize that this is an ideal that does not always work according to the original plans and intentions. Therefore divorce, as a last resort, is acceptable and so is second marriage to another. It is the compassion of Jesus rather than any sense of legalism that is rightly applied to the people involved in such emotionally difficult situations.

One final thought on this incident concerning the Law of Moses and the matter of divorce: were the Pharisees really interested in Jesus' knowledge of the Law, or was there something else at work? Just as the Pharisees would later [in Mark 12] try to trick Jesus over the issue of paying taxes to Caesar or to God, I am sure that the purpose of this testing over divorce was much more to do with trying to trap Jesus into publicly criticizing King Herod Antipas and his adulterous relationship with his brother's wife than it was a test of his knowledge of Mosaic Law. Just imagine:

"If only we can get Jesus to fall for our test – we can report it to Herod and the head of Jesus will be on the platter just as the head of John the Baptist had been!"

And so they go to Jesus. "Jesus, let us ask you a question. Is it lawful for a man to divorce his wife?"

Jesus replies, "The Law of Moses condemns divorce."

"Ah ha! So what have you got to say about King Herod Antipas and his new wife?"

This is all a continuation of the plot to kill Jesus, agreed between the Pharisees and the followers of Herod Antipas recorded back in Mark 3:5-7. No wonder Jesus is supposed to have called the Pharisees hypocrites, blind guides, whitewashed tombs, snakes and even a brood of vipers [Matthew 23]! Marriage is the ideal. Divorce may be the lesser of competing evils. But the subject of Mosaic marriage and divorce was not really what the Pharisees came to discuss with Jesus!

Cohabiting couples and single-sex partnerships

But where does all this leave us when discussing issues today such as cohabiting couples and single-sex partnerships? I take the line that the creation of a marriage through thc 'two becoming one flesh' is not the result of either a formal church service or a wedding ceremony in a registrar's (justice of the peace's) office. The 'two becoming one flesh' is the result of a positive commitment to a life-long partnership, freely entered into by the consenting people (be they male and female; female and female, or male and male) that will be faithful, monogamous and loving.

The compassion of Jesus applies to all coming together, and also, if it becomes inevitable, in the separating of the partnerships in divorce. My hope is that the day will come soon when single-sex marriages will be blessed with either a church or registrar's office formal wedding ceremony, and that all divorce and remarriage will be dealt with compassionately by the whole Church just as it is by the State.

This whole section of teaching on the family that began at Mark 9:36 comes to an end with a repetition of those references to children [Mark 10:13-16]. It is a simple literary devise to indicate where a block of the narrative begins and ends.

However, in the arrangement of the narrative of Mark's Gospel there are three other stories to bring this section to a close. The first links family with riches and the cost of discipleship. It concerns a rich young man who is serious about following Jesus but who is not prepared to give up all that he has to follow the man from Galilee [Mark 10:17-31]. Once again the message here is not that money and riches are wrong in themselves, but the issues are how we achieved these in the first place and, even more importantly, as to how we use them for the common good.

The second [Mark 10:32-34] is Jesus telling his disciples once again that he will soon be killed in Jerusalem. Did Jesus really warn his disciples to expect the worst or is this another case of reading the events back into the history of that fateful journey into Jerusalem to make sense of the execution of Jesus? Perhaps this is another logos incident that was developed into a mythos explanation?

The third story concerns James and John and their request to take the most important seats in the Kingdom of God [Mark 10:35-45]:

> Then James and John, the sons of Zebedee, came to him. "Teacher," they said, "we want you to do for us whatever we ask."

[Mark 10:35 (New International Version)]

What impudence of these two upstart fishermen to demand anything of Jesus! These two brothers went to Jesus, not so much with a question, a petition or a prayer, but they went with a demand: "we want you to do for us whatever we ask."

I wonder if the brothers were open to negotiation or perhaps they would not take 'no' as an answer? Until recently, my reaction to this demand from these brothers was usually one of surprised indignation: the audacity of two upstart fishermen to command whatever of Jesus!

And yet, when I consider how, in years gone by, I have often phrased intercessory prayers I begin to realize that I am little different to James and John. Think about our prayers for others. Do we ask anything in the name of Jesus believing that it will happen just as we ask? Or do we qualify our asking just in case our God does not appear to answer our wishes as we wish them with the catchall phrase, '… but according to your will'?

When we do not get the answer that we prayed for do we contort our thinking to try to excuse God or to explain God's actions? Or perhaps our praying is so fervent that it appears that we are demanding our God to do things just as we ask them – no negotiation and no excuse on God's part?

This raises all kinds of questions about the nature of God and the purpose of prayer. If God is the all-powerful being who intervenes in life, answering the prayers of some and ignoring or reversing the prayers of others; heaping blessings upon some and allowing others to die in tsunami, flood, earthquake, car crashes, oncology wards and so on: then perhaps this God can be bargained with? Or perhaps our persistent prayers, to the point of boring our God, can change the mind of this Supreme Being?

After all, the Hebrew Testament contains stories of numerous people who have argued with their Yahweh God, trying to understand the actions and to change the mind of their God over certain issues.

Abraham, a man with the Rottweiler instinct

One of the most interesting characters in the Hebrew Testament as far as I am concerned is Abraham. He was a man with the Rottweiler instinct: once he had his teeth into something he was reluctant to let it go without a fight. Abraham, a man like so many of us, so often got it badly wrong. Yet, in the stories, he had the audacity and the courage to argue with his God. After all, what is the difference between pleading one's case and arguing with another? Perhaps it is only a matter of degree?

Genesis Chapter 18 has Abraham pleading and arguing with his God over the fate of the cities of Sodom and Gomorrah, threatened with destruction by his God. Then in Genesis Chapter 32 verses 24-31 there is the story of Jacob, not just arguing with God but physically fighting with God!

> 24So Jacob was left alone, and a man wrestled with him till
> daybreak. 25When the man saw that he could not overpower
> him, he touched the socket of Jacob's hip so that his hip was
> wrenched as he wrestled with the man. 26Then the man said,
> "Let me go, for it is daybreak."
> But Jacob replied, "I will not let you go unless you bless me."
> 27The man asked him, "What is your name?"
> "Jacob," he answered.
> 28Then the man said, "Your name will no longer be Jacob, but Israel, because you have struggled with God and with humans and have overcome."
> 29Jacob said, "Please tell me your name."
> But he replied, "Why do you ask my name?" Then he blessed him there.
> 30So Jacob called the place Peniel, saying, "It is because I saw God face to face, and yet my life was spared."

> [31]The sun rose above him as he passed Peniel, and he was limping because of his hip. (New International Version)

The Book of Job is all about arguing Job's case with his friends and with his God. In Chapter 13 in particular we find Job trying to understand why such calamity has fallen upon him even though he considers that he has done nothing wrong to deserve such treatment from his God. Verses 20-24 are heartrending calls from deep within Job, and who can read them even today and not be touched by the depth of his despair?

> [20]Only grant me these two things, God, and then I will not hide from you:
> [21]Withdraw your hand far from me, and stop frightening me with your terrors.
> [22]Then summon me and I will answer, or let me speak, and you reply to me.
> [23]How many wrongs and sins have I committed? Show me my offense and my sin.
> [24] Why do you hide your face and consider me your enemy? (New International Version)

It is there again in the Book of Isaiah. My favorite chapter is 43 [attributed to Second Isaiah], which has those wonderful statements in verses 18 and 19 that can be so easily cherry-picked, but even so, applied to the situation in the Church and in the world today:

> [18]Forget the former things; do not dwell on the past.
> [19]See, I am doing a new thing! Now it springs up; do you not perceive it? I am making a way in the wilderness and streams in the wasteland.
> (New International Version)

But in that same chapter, verse 26, according to Second Isaiah's understanding there is an invitation from his God, "Review the past for me, let us argue the matter together; state the case for your innocence." (New International Version)

So if God is an intervening force for good or ill, maybe the two brothers, James and John, were not so wrong after all? Perhaps they were merely continuing in that Jewish tradition that we Christians seem to have lost – the audacity and the courage to argue with our God?

Perhaps that is how those who pray to an interventionist God should petition for healing and wholeness? Not with nice quiet prayers of "... if it be your will..." but full-blooded arguing prayers of "What's the purpose of allowing this to happen at all?"

But if our understanding of God is not that of the ancient of days, of the interventionist God who, with fickleness, blesses some and curses others, then the wrestling of Jacob and the pleading of Abraham, Job, Second Isaiah, James and John, and even of ourselves in our prayers for others – then arguing with this kind of God is from another time and another place with little relevance to life today.

Prayers of intercession

My prayers of intercession during times of public worship are constructed around an introductory statement or phrase followed by silence for each one to pray in whatever way they find appropriate and to whatever image or experience of God they have. This allows those who believe in an interventionist God to pray – even to argue their case on behalf of others for God to intervene.

And for the growing number of followers of the Jesus Way with whom I come into contact through my ministry on and beyond the edge of the Church, the silence within the times of intercessory prayers allows the opportunity to silently center one's self upon the sacredness of life itself and one's role in living God's Kingdom in this present time.

There is a second point that strikes me about these two disciples: they were important to Jesus and to the Jesus enterprise. They were poor but not without means. Mark 1:20 intimates that their father owned a fishing boat so there was some kind of business going on. According to the story there were hired men left in the boat with their father when James and John left to follow Jesus.

Thirdly, Mark 3:17 goes on to name James and John as "sons of thunder" – presumably because they had booming voices or because they argued a great deal – or both! But, sadly, they also had an over-inflated self-estimation of their own importance.

But notice that they had only just heard Jesus talking about being the first and the last; about the greatest in the Kingdom being the least important – the servants of all. Yet still they failed to understand what Jesus and his Kingdom teaching was all about. They were still thinking that power and political position, rank and status were the marks of great office in God's Kingdom. As I look at the pomp and ceremony in some Christian Churches, and at the way some followers seem to worship their leaders, I think that little has changed over the intervening two millennia!

Fourthly, notice how their self-inflation angered the other disciples. But I wonder if any of them had reacted angrily because they had really heard, received and understood the Kingdom teaching of Jesus any better than James and John had done? Was their anger because they wanted to be appointed to the very places on the left and right of Jesus that the two brothers had had the courage or the impudence to request for themselves?

Perhaps it was a rebuke of the two brothers because the other disciples were still thinking in a similar way owing to their own misunderstanding of the nature of the agape servant of the Kingdom?

Last, consider how Jesus responded. To the brothers it was in a calm challenge that said, "To sit at my right or left is not for me to grant. These places belong to those for whom they have been prepared."

This is a little tongue-in-cheek but if I need evidence to reassure me that Jesus was a Methodist at heart, then it is here in this story! His response to the other disciples was to call a meeting to repeat his teaching of the Kingdom all over again. Oh the infinite patience of Jesus towards his followers!

I wonder how often Jesus had to say to himself, "How long will it be before they learn and understand what my vision of God's Kingdom is all about in the here and now?"

I also wonder how often the Jesus Spirit is asking the same question as it broods and moves within the Church and its members today: "How long will it be before they learn and understand that the Jesus vision of God's Kingdom is not about reciting creeds and doctrines but it is about relational servant-hood in the here and now?"

We Christians are too nice.

We Christians are too nice. As we look at the state of the world and at the:

• 6,000,000 Palestinians living in refugee camps outside the Israeli borders (NB a similar number to those Jews killed in Nazi death camps);

• The ongoing war in Afghanistan with no apparent exit strategy;

• Thousands dying as a result of earthquakes, tsunami, floods and other natural disasters;

• The poorest in the world being the first to suffer as a result of our catastrophic abuse of the earth's climate.

As we look at these we should be angry with ourselves. We should be angry with our governments sitting on the Goldstone fence. We should be angry with 'God' for allowing the nonsense argument of free will to allow such enormous pain and suffering.

Let us stop being nice Christians and be angry to the point of doing more than we are doing now. Let us be angry and argue with whatever we understand 'God' to be. Let us be like Abraham and Job; Jacob; James and John. And in the actions of our anger let us become people of compassionate action as servants of all.

Blind Bartimaeus – a fictional character

The next section in the Mark narrative now moves to Jericho [10:46-52] with the story of blind Bartimaeus, the son of Timaeus, receiving his sight. This story is both selected and placed to immediately contrast the attitudes and extraordinary demands of James and John. Bartimaeus was blind and desperate for healing. He did not demand anything of Jesus. All he did was to call out to attract the attention of Jesus as he and his entourage walked past on their way out of Jericho. Doubtless Bartimaeus had heard the stories of the wisdom teacher who also had the power to heal, and he desperately wanted some of that healing for himself. But, unlike James and John, he did not have the audacity to command – only to draw the attention of Jesus to him as he sat behind the crowds, hidden from the view of Jesus.

Consider what Mark records Bartimaeus as having called out: "Son of David, have mercy on me!" Bartimaeus did not call out "Son of God" or "Son of Man", but "Son of David."

There are seven references in the Christian Testament to Jesus being "Son of David". Mark uses this title twice, Matthew uses it three times and Luke twice. However, Jesus cannot be the direct son of David because the two Gospels that have a genealogy of Jesus have him separated from David by almost 1000 years.

Matthew has 26 generations between Jesus and David, while Luke lists 41 generations – and they both cannot be right! There is also a problem with Matthew's counting. Matthew 1:17 states that there were "fourteen generations… from David to the exile to Babylon, and fourteen from the exile to the Christ." Unlike our counting systems, Matthew seems to have included, at either end, both David and Jesus in his calculations!

But the differences between these genealogies of Matthew and

Luke are not historically important. These genealogies were not intended to be accurate documented history. All they were doing was demonstrating the belief of the writers that Jesus was descended from King David. They were hindsight statements of faith linking Jesus to the Hebrew prophetic expectations of the coming of the long-promised Messiah who would be a descendent, that is a distant son of David.

The call of Bartimaeus, "Jesus, Son of David, have mercy on me!" is probably Peter's interpretation of history, linking his first-hand experiences of Jesus with his developing awareness that Jesus was indeed the Messianic 'Son of David'. As such, the meeting between Bartimaeus and Jesus at this Jericho gateway does not need to be a factually accurate report of an historical event that may or may not have taken place.

Indeed, although it is an off the wall speculation on my part, it is possible that Bartimaeus, son of Timaeus, never existed and this incident at a Jericho gate never happened. If we simply read Mark's Gospel at face value, and especially if we read it as literal fact and as accurate history, we are ignoring the all-important context in which it was written. Worse still, such a literal reading is tearing out the very heart of what Peter and Mark were trying to convey.

To help explain my reasoning concerning the non-existence of blind Bartimaeus I invite you to use your imagination. Come with me to Rome where we find Peter and Mark having just visited a theatrical production of a dialogue written almost 400 years before. It is Cicero's Latin translation from the pen of the Greek philosopher Plato. The dialogue is called 'Timaeus' and features a conversation mainly between Socrates and a friend called Timaeus. Notice the link with Bartimaeus, the son of Timaeus – could this be Mark's way of simply meaning that his story was the 'son' of the Plato story 'Timaeus'?

The dialogue explores deep issues of life and eternity. As Peter watches so the pennies continue to fall into place concerning Jesus as Messiah God and his place in the nature of eternal issues. Peter watches as Plato's dialogue has Timaeus exploring the differences between the physical world and the eternal world. The creation of the physical world was based upon the orderliness of the heavens. The former is experienced through the senses and can be corrupted and will eventually pass away, but the latter is always the perfect constant, from time immemorial to time never-ending. Timaeus then makes the point that God is the creator of both the heavens and the earth, declaring that order is preferable to disorder.

Here is Peter the Jew, having earlier experienced Jesus the Jew as the great but failed reformer of Judaism, finding more links between Jesus and God as he feels the Ways of Jesus in his own life: ways that seem to bring order to his life being lived in the religious and political disorder of the Jews and Christians within the Roman Empire. For Peter, here is Jesus, of this world by birth but also of the eternal by virtue of being that long-expected Son of David – the Messiah.

In Peter's developing theology he experiences God as the foundation of order and Jesus as the embodiment of that heavenly order on earth. Therefore to Peter and to Mark, the coded message is that the orderly Jesus Way of the Messiah is preferable to the disorderly oppression and persecution of Jew and gentile followers of Jesus perpetrated by Rome. But neither Peter nor Mark can say or write such a thing, especially during a time of persecution. Therefore their declaration that Jesus is God is hidden within the Bartimaeus narrative.

There is something else of importance to notice about the name 'Timaeus'. It is not a Hebrew name but a Greek name meaning 'honored'! Therefore, Bartimaeus can be translated as 'son of the honored'. If all my speculation is correct then Bar Timaeus – Son of Timaeus – may well be nothing more than a Peter/Mark fictional creation to convey the deep truth of the experience of the Jesus Spirit with them in their adversity. I repeat, in my opinion, Mark's narrative was designed to hide the developing theologies concerning Jesus as God from the Roman oppressors.

Of course, Bartimaeus, son of Timaeus, could have been real and actually sat at the gate of Jericho and one day had called out to Jesus. But it is also possible that Mark's intention of including this story of Bartimaeus is more to do with a coded reassurance to the persecuted followers of the Jesus Way that Jesus and not Caesar was both Messiah and God, bringing a new order to their persecuted lives.

Be that as it may: notice also that in Mark's story Bartimaeus adds, "have mercy on me!" Mercy is about compassion, pity, sympathy and understanding. Whatever the story of Bartimaeus was originally about, the message being conveyed to the early followers of the Jesus Way residing in Rome was that to experience Jesus was, and remained, a personal experience of compassion, pity, sympathy and understanding. These were also the marks that set apart this Christian community of Jew and gentile alike from the excesses of Emperor Nero.

Bartimaeus called, "Jesus, have compassion on me..."

Jesus heard and called him over. Jesus asked, "What do you want me to do for you?"

The blind man said, "Rabbi, I want to see."

Neither James nor John needed to sit on the right or the left of Jesus in glory. Their demand had been one of personal greed rather than need. However, unlike James and John, whose demands were gently rebuffed by Jesus, blind Bartimaeus made his demand out of personal need. The demand of Bartimaeus, "I want to see", was called out of his great need to be able to see again. Jesus responded positively to his need whereas he never accepted greed as a reason for his favorable response. "Go, your faith has healed you."

It never ceases to amaze me that the qualities of love offered by ordinary people in ways of compassion, pity, sympathy and understanding greatly assist the process of healing and wholeness. Perhaps this is what this story of blind Bartimaeus is really all about? That the followers of the Jesus Way should be honorable people who serve those who are in genuine need using the greatest weapon of all at our disposal – the unconditional accepting love that offers compassion, pity, sympathy and understanding. To live in this way is to live the way of honor and the Jesus Way. It is the way of humanity. It does not discriminate between being Buddhist, Christian, Hindu, Jew, Muslim, Sikh or whatever for these qualities of love are universal. To live this way will change us and the world about us because it is the sacred way that is common to all the great religions of the world.

It was in Jesus of Nazareth that Peter first experienced such fullness of humanity. It was also through Peter's community that Mark probably first experienced the sacredness of the Jesus Spirit. It is still that way today, so that the Jesus Spirit lived by the community of followers of the Jesus Way is where others (and we) will experience more of the sacred. It is where the depth of humanity will bless others and us. It is there in that humanity that they and we will also experience divinity.

Mark Chapter 11:
The Triumphal Entry into Jerusalem

We will return to the theatre analogy a little later but now the Mark narrative takes us to the gates of Jerusalem where we find the triumphal entry of Jesus into the city [Mark 11:1-11]. But I have many problems with the traditional understanding of the events of that Palm Sunday and of that fateful week in Jerusalem. How many sermons have you heard over the years telling that Jesus exercised his supernatural foreknowledge to locate the place where a foal of a donkey would be tied?

How often have you wondered how the owner of the foal could simply let the animal go without payment – simply because the disciples said, "The Master has need of it – he will return it quickly"?

Would you let your car go simply because a couple of men said to you, "The Master has need of it – he will return it quickly"? If so, I'm in the market for a bright red Porsche 911!

How often have you been left with the impression that the entry of Jesus into Jerusalem was accompanied by a huge crowd welcoming Jesus with shouts of "Hosanna" as he rode through the city streets on his way to the Temple?

How often have you thought that this triumphal entry was a huge demonstration and a disruption of ordinary life of the people of Jerusalem as Jesus and His disciples marched by?

How often have you seen in your imagination the Palm Sunday boldness of Jesus and his disciples that seemed to frighten the scribes and the Pharisees and somehow challenged the Roman authorities to step aside in fear of the reaction of the people who, in their thousands, were welcoming Jesus and His companions and followers?

How often have you imagined the ordinary people of Jerusalem who were expecting the Messiah to come leading an army against the Roman occupiers riding on the back of a horse, the symbol of the warrior king, suddenly and inexplicably changing their expectations and warmly welcoming the Messiah riding on the back of a foal of a donkey? To some the donkey was an animal of derision and to others a symbol of those people of little social or political importance. How often have you been told that Jesus rode through the city right into the Temple and immediately turned over the tables of the sellers and the moneylenders?

How often have you been given the impression that this was probably the first time Jesus had been back to Jerusalem since he was allegedly left behind in the Temple at the age of 12? Well, of course, all of this might have been the way that it was. But, to me, there are too many unanswered questions and contradictions in this simple face value acceptance of the events of that Palm Sunday.

When one begins to consider the geography and the events of the time, perhaps a different picture may emerge? Contrary to some interpretations, Jesus and his band of disciples had been together in the area of Jerusalem before. According to the Gospel records they had visited Bethany on more than one occasion to stay at the home of Martha, Mary and Lazarus.

Bethany was less than five miles to the east of Jerusalem near the Mount of Olives. Therefore I cannot see how a devote Jew such as Jesus, one who had stood up and taught in the synagogues and who had been called 'rabbi', could visit friends less than a two hours' walk from Jerusalem and not venture into the great city especially when it held such an important place in the plans of the Jewish God Yahweh and in the childhood memories of Jesus.

How could Jesus resist travelling into Jerusalem on the occasions when he was visiting Mary, Martha and Lazarus in Bethany? There were so many memories for Jesus and so many plans for the future. To my way of thinking, it is more than probable that Jesus had already met with the owner of the donkey either in the village of Bethany or Bethphage and arranged for the animal to be released to him for a couple of hours sometime in the near future.

May be that was why the owner did not ask for payment or why he did not refuse the disciples when they went to him and said, “The Lord has need of it and will send it back here immediately.” It is quite possible that the disciples were somewhat terrified of the prospect of entering triumphantly into Jerusalem where the Roman army would accept no show of resistance and would not allow any group to stir up the populace and incite them to rise against the Romans.

It is also quite possible that the strewing of the way with palm branches happened only on the road from Bethany to the outskirts of Jerusalem where the disciples cut the palm branches from those trees that lined the road. There the disciples would have been bold enough to place them onto the road in the knowledge that they were still hidden by the trees from the Roman soldiers in the city of Jerusalem.

It is possible that, by this time, the crowd actually numbered little more than the dozen disciples and their immediate friends like Mary, Martha and Lazarus. Perhaps that was why the Romans were not interested in the progress of the ‘triumphal’ march because they knew nothing about it?

And when the small band reached the edge of the city wall – what then? In all four Gospels, Jesus approached Jerusalem from the east from the direction of Bethany and Bethphage. If they actually went into the city streets they would have had to make a detour from the Bethany to Jerusalem road adding an extra mile to the north, into the Bezetha part of the city. From there it was only 100 yards through the city into the Temple through the Sheep Gate.

Or they could have gone an extra 1.5 miles to the south entering the Lower City and parading a further 150 yards through the streets and into the Temple through the Huldah Gates. Or they could have entered directly into the Temple on the shortest route from Bethany and never needed to go into the streets of Jerusalem or encounter the opposition of the Roman soldiers. Now, had you been there in that group of disciples, which route would you have chosen?

I know which one I would have taken – the one of least resistance and the shortest in time and distance, especially as this was not the only 'triumphal' parade into Jerusalem on that day. Crossan and Borg [2008] tell us that there were two rival parades into Jerusalem: Jesus on the donkey from the east, as a man declaring the power of love and social justice that are the essence of the Kingdom of God, while from the west came Pilate and his cohorts, parading the opposite vision, that of Imperial Rome with all its love of power.

Then, according to Mark, having had a quick look in the Temple Jesus took his followers back that night to Bethany to stay in the home of Mary, Martha and Lazarus. Note, however, the similar account in Matthew 21:12 and Luke 19:45 has Jesus turning over the tables of the moneychangers there and then on Palm Sunday.

It was only on their return to Jerusalem the next day that, according to Mark's Gospel [11:12-19], Jesus caused the problems with the moneychangers and sellers in the Temple. En route Jesus is said to have cursed a fig tree because it was full of leaves but had no fruit – not surprising as Mark records that it was not the season for figs! How odd.

Only with the outburst in the Temple did the Temple authorities feel threatened by his actions and accusations against them. But no matter what actually happened on that Palm Sunday or on the Monday the truth for me, as a follower of the Jesus Way, is that Jesus had set his face to go to Jerusalem to challenge the authorities that were abusing and degrading the Kingdom of God.

The Jesus agenda: social, political and religious reformation

His was a social, political and religious reform movement. He was primarily concerned with social justice based upon his understanding that the absolute love that is God was an affront to the evil ways of humankind manifesting in the Temple. Evil is always a challenge to the purity and goodness that are the results of implemented social justice. It was also only when this commotion was brought to the attention of the Roman soldiers and authorities that they were alerted to what Jesus was doing and saying.

It is important to remember that the emergent theology of the early Jewish Christian Church, as it struggled to make sense of the life and death of Jesus and of the continuing presence of the Jesus Spirit, only slowly developed links between Jesus and the Old Testament prophecies. For example:

• The Gospel of Mark was not written until some 30 years after the first Easter and it makes only 57 references that link the life, death and resurrection of Jesus to the Old Testament.

• Matthew's Gospel, written just before Luke's but written by a Jew for a predominantly Jewish audience makes 199 references to the Old Testament linking the life and death and resurrection of Jesus to Old Testament prophecies.

• Luke's Gospel, written some 20 to 30 years after Mark's Gospel makes 147 references to the Old Testament.

This example also demonstrates, at least to me, the continuing development of the Early Church understanding of Jesus beyond the initial Son of Man from Nazareth who was uniquely filled with God's Spirit, into the Christ, the Son of God.

It really doesn't bother me whether or not the events of Palm Sunday happened exactly as reported by Mark, Mathew or Luke. What matters to me is that the social justice message of Jesus is as much for today as it was for 2000 years ago. What matters is finding new ways of applying the truth of those events to our lives in the world today.

Then Mark presents the second part of the odd story of the withered fig tree that Jesus cursed because it was bearing no fruit, even out of season! Is this story simply an indication that Jesus was no horticulturist and therefore he did not recognize the season for figs? Or perhaps this is Mark using a logos comment by Jesus about a fig tree to illustrate the power of prayer? According to Mark, Jesus made prayer into a very powerful, almost magical tool. Even with the smallest faith in the world it was possible to move mountains by prayer.

However, I am convinced that neither Jesus nor Mark intended this to be a literal geological statement about what one is capable of achieving through believing in the power of prayer. Perhaps this was Mark offering a way out for those who might take this statement about the power of prayer too literally so that when they pray for mountains to move and they fail to shift, then the problem is not with prayer but with the pray-er who has retained some unforgiveness within their own lives? After all, Mark now says, "... when you stand praying, if you hold anything against anyone, forgive him, so that your Father in heaven may forgive you your sins."

But was this simply a metaphor concerning prayer? Borg and Crossan (2008) make a very strong case for this withering of the fig tree to be linked with the actions of Jesus when he overturned the tables and chased out those who were doing business in the Court of the Gentiles in the Jerusalem Temple. Borg and Crossan state that this action was not a cleansing of the Temple in the sense that all the moneychangers and sellers of animals and birds for ritual sacrifice were thieves and robbers. Pilgrims to the Temple depended upon these people and they were fully authorized to be going about their legitimate business.

This was a symbolic and prophetic action of Jesus linking right back some 600 years to Jeremiah who symbolically wore the yoke of oxen to say that it was better to surrender to the might of Babylon than to have everything destroyed by the Babylonian armies. And the prophetic message of Jeremiah was that if God's people put worship before justice then the people and the Temple would be destroyed.

Therefore, perhaps the outburst of Jesus in the Temple was not about cleansing it of robbers and thieves but was in fact symbolically re-enacting Jeremiah's message? Jesus was condemning the Temple authorities because they were so wrapped up in ritual and worship that they had forgotten that God does not require animal sacrifice but living and doing justice.

Jesus then returned once again to the Temple in Jerusalem [Mark 11:27-33] where the story is told of a confrontation with the chief priests, the teachers of the Law and the elders who went to him and asked, "By what authority are you doing these things? And who gave you authority to do this?"

The Temple confrontation

This Temple confrontation may or may not have happened quite as Mark recorded but it certainly made a good story for Mark's listeners! I can just imagine them sitting and listening to the unfolding narrative. I can see them nodding as old sages as they heard of the wisdom of Jesus, turning the tables and asking a question about their attitudes towards John the Baptist. And upon receiving an answer of, "We don't know," Jesus replied with a wry smile of satisfaction, "Neither will I tell you by what authority I am doing these things." I really do not think that this part of the narrative is anything other than a good oral storyteller's technique to encourage listener participation and identification with the 'mind pictures' of the incident created in the heads of the listeners.

Mark Chapter 12:
Jesus is confronted by the Temple Authorities

Mark's narrative now has Jesus launching into the telling of parables. The first [Mark 12:1-11] is more likely a 'with hindsight' oral story than a parable actually told by Jesus. It is much more a statement of what the early Christians believed happened to Jesus and to his Jewish persecutors. As they read back into the events of that first Easter so they were able to put prophetic words into the mouth of Jesus concerning the landowner being sent and then killed by the tenants. Eventually justice is done and the son is vindicated. The tenants are killed and the vineyard is given to others. This was early Christian doctrine for church communities whose membership was now less Jewish and more gentile:

• God had sent prophets in former times to warn the Chosen People to repent and to turn back to God, but they failed to listen to the prophets.

• Eventually God sent his only son because, God thought, the Chosen People would listen to him and respond as God wished.

• Sadly, the Chosen People took the only son (*Jesus*) and killed him.

The result was that God's anger was now turned in full measure against his Chosen People. The punishment was the destruction of the Temple and the mass suicide of Jewish fighters at Masada. [NB: this point would have been added later unless Mark's Gospel was written after 70 CE.]

This parable of the tenants is rounded off by another theological statement in verse 11: "The stone the builders rejected has become the capstone" and the whole of the future of the Christian Church could rest on Jesus holding the edifice in place, stone upon stone finally finished by the capstone! This is theology, not history, although at some point Jesus may well have told stories that were variations on confrontations between absentee landlords and their tenants. There were many of both, and perhaps in the earlier logos events of Jesus he was much more on the side of the exploited tenants than he was on the side of the absentee landlords, who were getting rich on the backs of the poor who scraped a living on fields and in vineyards that were not their own.

Mark then ties this parable of the tenants into the logos events of that final week in Jerusalem: the chief priests, the teachers of the Law and the elders looked for a way to arrest him. It was the storyteller's technique then to do what any police crime thriller does today: it identifies the motivation, offers the opportunity and then shows that the deed is done. Here we have Mark telling Peter's story of the motivation of the chief priests *et al* to kill Jesus; the opportunity would soon be presented and the deed would be successfully carried out. And all this told in retrospect with that valuable gift of writer's hindsight!

The motivation has been stated and now the Mark narrative moves us to yet another opportunity presenting itself to the Pharisees and Herodians. In Mark 12:13-17 these so-called leaders of the people attempted to dupe Jesus into either refusing to acknowledge Caesar, the penalty for which would be arrest for civil disobedience, or worse, he would be seen as rejecting Yahweh God, the intended result being that the faithful Jews would turn against Jesus. Either way the Pharisees and Herodians would be free of Jesus once and for all.

Too often this story is taken at face value and when this happens a valuable historic point is missed, one that is far more vital than a debate concerning paying taxes, affairs of state and religion. In fact, the roots of this story can be traced back some 600 years before Jesus to the Babylonian exile.

At that time the exiled Jewish leadership established a new ethnic 'front line' that isolated the exiles from their Babylonian captors. Their laws and commandments were written down to help them avoid being assimilated into the Babylonian way of life. The underlying message to the exiles was that this was a temporary event and their God, Yahweh, as the only true God would one day set them free. However, the condition was that they had to keep themselves apart from the Babylonians. To assimilate would thwart the plans of Yahweh and the Hebrews would disappear altogether. It was this ethnic 'front line' that was at the root of the question, "Is it lawful to pay taxes to Caesar or not?"

As I read the Gospels I see Jesus developing out of a strict Pharisaic code of holiness by separation into an understanding of the love of Yahweh being inclusive. He broke down barriers between Jew and gentile, female and male, treating all people as equals. Jesus understood that Yahweh [a] did not take the side of the Jews against the gentiles and [b] no one tribe could claim sole ownership of or access to God. (Jack Spong continues to be one of my contemporary theological heroes and has three excellent chapters on the approach of Jesus to breaking prejudices, stereotypes, and tribal and religious boundaries in his outstanding book *Jesus for the Non-Religious*.)

In 1952 the Bible translator, writer and clergyman, J.B. Phillips, wrote a book entitled *Your God is Too Small*. Although the book is now outdated, the more I study the Hebrew and Christian Scriptures the more convinced I become that the Jewish understandings of God at the time of Jesus were way too small. It was within the early Christian communities, including Jews and gentiles, that the Hebrew exclusive understanding of Yahweh was expanded as a result of the teaching and ministry of Jesus. For open and progressive Christians, Jesus is the gateway into the awareness of the sacred but he is not the only gateway. Other gateways exist for other religious faiths. For any faith group to restrict 'God' to the followers of their own religious experiences and explanations is to make God too small!

I remind you that I cannot and I will not tell you what is the Jesus Way for you. All I can do is explain my experiences of Jesus that have become my way of following his example. In my encounter with the sacred met in Jesus I am called to challenge all unnecessary boundaries that separate people from people and nations from nations. As I look at our contemporary world I often wonder what future there may be for any of us if we do not live the boundary-breaking life of Jesus and challenge the barriers created by cultural, economic, political and religious tribalism.

It is vitally important for me to go beyond the face value of the question from the Pharisees concerning paying taxes to Caesar and to live the message of Jesus in today's world. This passage is not really about the creative work of accountants but about challenging injustice and inequality wherever the poor are:

• Denied cheap anti-malaria or HIV/AIDs medicines because government and non-governmental agencies are corrupting and exploiting the system.

• Driven out of business because 'their' fish stocks are permitted to be taken by huge factory fishing fleets or where EU and US surplus food is dumped onto poor countries in the guise of 'charity'.

• Exploited by the big coffee importers and main high street stores that are making a fortune out of every single cup of coffee sold at the expense of the poor growers of the coffee beans.

• Impoverished by lack of education and unfair employment practices in which both child and adult labor are paid a meager amount in sweatshops producing consumer goods that are then sold at a huge profit in Western shops.

• Made to fear stepping outside their own homes after dark owing to the threat of mugging or worse.

• Physically and psychologically damaged by war and its often-unwelcome companion, the evil of collateral damage.

- Trampled on by the politics of the state.

These are examples of what drives me to get involved and to do something, no matter how little, about injustice and inequality. In this context I quote John Wesley's Rule for Christian Living:

> Do all the good you can
> By all the means you can
> In all the ways you can
> In all the places you can
> At all the times you can
> To all the people you can
> As long as ever you can.

And to live by that rule will be truly boundary breaking. It is the key to the future for all humanity.

Next in the developing narrative [12:18-27] Peter/Mark has the Sadducees going again to Jesus. They did not believe in the resurrection and I doubt that the Sadducees went to Jesus to discuss the issue of marriage in heaven. They had ulterior motives, not only attempting to trick Jesus into undermining himself before their own supporters but this was, perhaps, a sly kick at King Herod who probably did not subscribe to their stance on the resurrection? After all, Herod was alarmed that Jesus was John the Baptist returning to haunt him.

The 'black widow'

Here is a long Sadducean story concerning a poor unfortunate 'black widow' who married a man who then died before she had any children. According to the Law of Moses, a childless widow was to marry a brother of the deceased and any children born from that relationship would be deemed to be the children of the first husband. Sadly this second brother died before any children were born therefore the Law of Moses came into play once again. This happened seven times and the last brother died without this poor woman giving birth to any child for the first or for any of the husbands. The trick question that came at the end of the story was, "At the resurrection whose wife will she be, since the seven were married to her?" [verse 23] The response of Jesus was a challenge to these Temple leaders for not knowing either the Scriptures or the power of God.

From this story it seems to me that both Peter and Mark believed that Jesus accepted some form of life beyond death. After all they have Jesus comment, "When the dead arise." However, according to this story, the life beyond was not going to be a repeat of life on this earth. There would be no marriage and no one would be given in marriage. Whatever life beyond this one is all about, it is not simply a repeat with all the blemishes, pain and suffering removed. It is a wonderful picture but, according to Jesus, it is not like that in reality.

As Jesus developed his reply he referenced right back to Moses and the story of meeting God in the burning bush. As Temple leaders the Sadducees should have known the implications of the Law of Moses but Jesus accused them of being in error. This was not so much because they denied the reality of resurrection but because the way in which they conducted both their lives and their Judaism they had missed the central point: "God is not the God of the dead, but of the living." [verse 27]

Once again this is a good storyteller's technique, dropping into the text a phrase, sentence or idea that would be reoccurring and is, in fact, the pivotal message that the reader will suddenly realize has been the golden thread running throughout. The core of the pivotal sentence would be raised again inside the empty tomb, "You are looking for Jesus the Nazarene, who was crucified. He has risen! He is not here." [Mark 16:6] No matter what stories Peter chose to tell and Mark selected to write down, this is the crux of the whole

Gospel summed up in these 12 words: "God is not the God of the dead, but of the living."

The resurrection of Jesus is a present tense activity

Once again, the resurrection of Jesus is not something just from the past, and we waste much time if we merely seek it at some time in the future. The vital issue is that the resurrection of Jesus is a present tense activity to be lived by the followers of the Jesus Way on a daily basis: God is not the God of the dead, but of the living.

What a wonderful message to all of us and for the world out there in which so many people are seeking a spirituality that is increasingly bypassing the Christian Church. In my opinion the time has come for the Church to stop looking back to its ancient creeds and doctrines – those are of the dead – and instead take the risk of becoming something new, even if that means dying to its present form and organization.

We now come to another of the confrontations recorded by Mark that happened in the final week of the life of Jesus. Here Mark demonstrates that not every Pharisee or Sadducee was out to get Jesus. In Mark 12:28-34 one of the teachers of the Law is listening to this debate with the Sadducees. Impressed with the answer that Jesus gave, this newcomer asks a genuine question. "Of all the commandments, which is the most important?"

Jesus replies with not one but two commands, "Love God and love your neighbor." Notice how the questioner responds, "You are correct." This man who is steeped in religious rules and regulations has a converting moment standing there in the presence of Jesus: simply believing what the religious leaders and traditions pronounce as the only practice and the only truth can be stumbling blocks to discerning and experiencing God.

All the rules, regulations, traditions, doctrines and creeds of any religion are nothing unless they are continually subordinated to living the Golden Rule of compassionate sacrificial love that puts God and the genuine needs of others before one's own needs and desires. It is this Golden Rule that is common to all the great religions of the world. It is in living the Golden Rule that we truly experience God.

It is in our practicing self-sacrificial love towards all with whom we come into contact that we will find the liberty and the abundant love and life that the Jesus Spirit offers to us all. As I understand it, this is the Gospel of Jesus. This is the good news of the abundant life that Jesus constantly and willingly gave away so that his life and the lives of others could be transformed and renewed. This is what will change you and me and all people, that we love God with all our heart, soul, mind and strength and love others as much as we love ourselves.

In such abundant, compassionate sacrificial love of others there is liberty and the only real personal experience of God that matters. Jesus responded to this religious leader with warmth, "You are not far from the kingdom of God."

And now, like many good stories, the storyteller has set that warm glow created in the preceding episode of the affirmative discussion between Jesus and the religious leader, only to be followed by another confrontation in which Jesus, the protagonist, is expected to emerge the victor.

The teachers of the Law are not all like the one who has just shared so positively and genuinely with Jesus. Here [Mark 12:35-40] Jesus addresses the crowd as he picks up the challenge of the other teachers that the Christ should be the son of David. It is a complex argument that takes the story back to Psalm 110:1:

> The LORD said to my Lord, 'Sit at my right hand, until I make your enemies into a footstool for your feet.' (New International Version)

If David was indeed the author of Psalm 110 then he recognized two Lords. One must have been Yahweh God and the other? It was something of a source of discomfort for the teachers of the Law standing by and observing. This gave great pleasure to the crowds who were listening adoringly to whatever Jesus was saying. These teachers of the Law were the high and mighty who were pleased to draw attention to themselves by wearing their fine elegant robes and expecting to be greeted in the marketplaces by the 'common' people.

These were also the same men who prayed long prayers to impress. They took the principal seats in the synagogues, as well as the places of honor at the religious feasts. The crowd was delighted as these 'sing your own praises' leaders were brought down to earth with a bump. As if to rub salt into a wound, Jesus continued to teach the people to be aware of the influence and the ways of these teachers of the Law.

And then comes another literary twist in the Mark narrative. Jesus says that these leaders, rather than protecting the poor and the widows, actually were exploiting these poor women, for which they will be punished. Mark has selected the story of the widow's mite [Mark 12:41-44] as a mirror to the appalling manipulative behavior of the teachers of the Law.

Whereas the rich put great amounts into the Temple treasury it came from their excess. But this poor widow, who needed every penny she could find, out of love for the Temple and for God put in everything that she had. Although the fraction of a penny was insignificant in monetary terms it was priceless in terms of love and devotion to God.

Jesus was underlining the cost of Kingdom living: it is not the total of what we give to others that really counts, but how much it really costs us to give of ourselves to others who are in need. Kingdom living is costly living but it is also grateful and joyful living.

Mark Chapter 13:
The Old Kingdom is coming to an end so the followers of Jesus are encouraged to be alert

The Old Kingdom of Christendom is coming to an end in this post-modern, secular and industrialized world. Therefore we have to find a way of engaging with this 'new' world so that we can continue to present the always relevant and contemporary Jesus Truth of loving God and loving one's neighbor; of doing to others what you wish them to do to you; that lasting peace does not come through violent victory in war but through the power of unconditional compassionate love.

Yet, out of those simple truths of Jesus, the institutional Church down the millennia has created a monolith that is rapidly getting to, if it has not already reached, its sell-by date. In Britain, Europe, North America, and Australasia the Church is undergoing a seismic collapse. Also in Britain, the 1990s were declared by the then Archbishop of Canterbury, George Carey, to be the Decade of Evangelism. Churches across the land developed and implemented outreach strategies based upon dressing up the traditional but increasingly threadbare dogmas of evangelical, institutional and traditional Christians. The result was that at the end of the 1990s there were fewer people attending Church than there had been at the beginning of the Decade of Evangelism.

Now, in Britain, it is the age of Fresh Expressions. This is the seeking of new ways of 'being and doing church' in the twenty-first century. This movement was set up jointly by the Church of England and the British Methodist Church in 2005 and built upon, to quote the Church of England Press Office on 12 February 2008, "firm biblical, theological and sociological foundations."

New ways of being Church are establishing across the land. Some have been very successful in attracting new worshippers: breakfast church; messy church; café church; and so on, leading in theory to what the present Archbishop of Canterbury, Dr. Rowan Williams, has described as a "mixed economy church" in which there will be the ancient core with a very loose fringe of new diverse communities of believers.

However, even though there are some really innovative strategies being introduced, in my experience and opinion, too many strategies are once again simply dressing up the old in new clothing. I fear that very soon we will probably see that many of these 'new suits of clothes' will be found wanting, reminiscent of Hans Christian Andersen's *The Emperor's New Clothes* in which the hoodwinked Emperor is found strutting around in his altogether…

But what has all that got to do with Mark 13:1-13? Consider that in the New International Version this passage is entitled "Signs of the end of the age" and in the New American Standard translation, "Things to come". Let me make it very clear, I am not into the eschatological end of the age theology when Jesus will return on the clouds to judge the living and the dead. However, I am convinced that we are already experiencing the signs of the end of the age of the institutional church in Britain, Europe, North America and Australasia. Even more worrying is that it is no longer a case of 'things to come' because they are here and impacting upon the institutional church already.

Fresh ways of being Church cannot start where we are and wishing that the world could become like us. The starting point has to be where the people 'out there' happen to be, living in a post-modern world, and that is where we need to be, both theologically and physically.

A genuine alternative to the 'old' dressed up as something fresh and new is an innovative Christian initiative called The Evangelism Project. This involves a group of people visiting different political and religious groups, not to evangelize but for themselves to be evangelized by their cultural insights and experiences! They go into the culture beyond the safety and comfort of their own beliefs and experiences to be taught and reformed by the way in which others experience and interpret life. The Project is based upon seeing the insights of others as profound gifts of personal and community transformation. Perhaps that is the attitude that the church needs to adopt in this post-modern world, so that we may better understand and interact by our living of the Kingdom in the midst of where the people happen to be? This is in line with the root verb of 'to teach' in both Hebrew and Greek - it is also the same word 'to learn'. In other words, to be evangelists today we need to allow ourselves to interact with and to be evangelized by the 'world' within which we live and work.

I make no apology if this is too challenging but it is not a shout of despair. It is a call to hope and to action. As churches we tend to spend too much time discussing what does not work and what we have tried in the past that has failed. Such talk is wasted talk. Rather, we should be identifying the good things that churches are already doing, and committing to doing them better still. And above all, when churches are considering ways in which they can be even more effective, they need to move on from the old ways of interpreting and understanding the Scriptures, as well as from the traditions of the Church. It needs to construct a future within the framework of the post-modern world in which we now live. If we can do that then I am sure that the best is yet to be!

Mark's Gospel [13:1-13] now continues with the stories of the warnings about impending disaster for both the Temple and the people. This has been dealt with in detail in *Setting Jesus Free* [pages 146-158] so suffice it for now to simply quote from pages 157/158:

> in a very real sense we are always living in the end times. The signs of the times – war, famine, deceit – are always similar and are always with us. But in spite of this, there is encouragement wherever we find our openness to the Spirit leading us to be more generous with ourselves and with others, within the bond of love in Jesus. Even though the signs of the times may be far from what we would like – nuclear proliferation, religious extremism, terrorism, and global climate change – the promise is sure in that as we love

> one another as demonstrated 2000 years ago by Jesus we will experience life in all its emotional, psychological and spiritual abundance. It is the economy of God's Kingdom that the more love we give away the more we will receive love.

Next comes a passage that I am persuaded concerns the desecration of the Temple in Jerusalem [Mark 13:14-23] in 70 CE. It seems to me that this passage is a follow on to the opening two verses of this chapter:

> [1]As Jesus was leaving the temple, one of his disciples said to him, "Look, Teacher! What massive stones! What magnificent buildings!" [2]"Do you see all these great buildings?" replied Jesus. "Not one stone here will be left on another; everyone will be thrown down."
> (New International Version)

The intervening verses elaborate the issue of the warnings and the signs of the times, but at this point Peter/Mark hid the real focus (*i.e. the Jerusalem Temple*) from their Roman oppressors by inviting readers and listeners themselves to decide what is the 'horrible thing' that is going to happen. This passage can be used to support the scholarship that says that Mark's Gospel was written in the aftermath of the destruction of the Jerusalem Temple and its desecration by the placing of busts of Roman 'God' Emperor in its courts. Alternatively, it was a 'with hindsight' addition some years after Mark had finished writing.

I still go with the 'with hindsight' addition, preferring the evidence that Peter was telling these stories of the impending destruction of the Temple, not because it had already happened (after all Peter was dead before that 'horrible thing' occurred) but because anyone with the slightest experience of the brutality meted out by Rome upon any who opposed the Empire knew that the rebellion that had broken out in Judea would have only one outcome.

The references as to what would happen when that 'horrible thing' came to pass are also alluding to earlier Judean writings. "If you are living in Judea at that time, run to the mountains" [verse 14] picks up the story concerning Judas Mattathias who was the first leader of the insurrection in 167 BCE against those Seleucid kings who not only persecuted the Jews but also desecrated ('the horrible thing') the Jerusalem Temple. This is told in 1 Maccabees 2:27-28 where Mattathias went throughout the city calling upon those people who were passionate about the law and who lived by the covenant to follow him. Then he ran away into the mountains taking with him his sons but they left all their possessions in the city.

Do not join the rebellion against Roman occupation

The Peter/Mark narrative then issued a warning that it was time to escape and not to join the rebellion against Roman occupation of Judea. There is an urgency to get out [Mark 13:15-20]: if anyone is on the roof of his house or working in the fields, run away from the devastation and destruction, and do not waste a moment going inside the house to collect any belongings: run away! Any pregnant women at that time would also be in terrible trouble because they may not have the physical strength to flee quickly enough from the Roman soldiers.

And Peter/Mark then said that the people should pray that this 'horrible thing' should not happen during the winter months because that would make both fleeing and its aftermath all the more difficult to cope with (additional proof, perhaps, that this was written before the 'horrible thing' in 70 CE?). The rebellion had started in Judea just as the persecution was in full swing in Rome, and things were so bad for the people of the synagogue and Temple that: "If the Lord doesn't make the time shorter, no one will be left alive." [verse 20 CEV] It is a shout of despair.

Maybe there were leaders of the revolt against Rome who were claiming to be the Messiah but Peter/Mark issued the warning that there would be false messiahs and false prophets promising to work miracles (e.g. the overthrow of Roman occupation in Judea) who would try to fool everybody, including those who were faithful to Jesus: "Be on your guard! That's why I am telling you these things now." [verses 21-23 CEV].

The narrative now offers comfort to those who are caught up in the persecution in Rome and the impact of Roman retaliation for rebellion in Judea:

> 24But in those days, following that distress, 'the sun will be darkened, and the moon will not give its light; 25the stars will fall from the sky, and the heavenly bodies will be shaken.' 26At that time people will see the Son of Man coming in clouds with great power and glory. 27And he will send his angels and gather his elect from the four winds, from the ends of the earth to the ends of the heavens.
> [Mark 13:24-27 (New International Version)]

But once again these are not original statements from the mouth of Peter or the pen of Mark. "The sun will become dark, and the moon will no longer shine" is a reference to Isaiah 13:10; Joel 2:10, 31 and 3.15; Ezekiel 32.7. Then again, "The stars will fall, and the powers in the sky will be shaken" is a quote from Isaiah 34:4 and Joel 2:10. Even the reference to "the Son of Man will be seen coming in the clouds with great power and glory" is in reality Daniel 13:26.

Mark 13:28-31 tells of lessons from the fig tree: people will know that summer is coming when its branches develop and start putting out foliage. It is a continuation of the theme of this chapter with the warnings that accompany the signs of the times. There is an additional element that suggests that Peter and Mark were both anticipating the imminent return of Jesus to release them from the horrors of Roman persecution: 30Truly I tell you, this generation will certainly not pass away until all these things have happened. [Mark 13:30 (New International Version)] This message of waiting and being alert for the return of Jesus is emphasized again in the closing six verses of Chapter 13.

Indeed, verse 36, with its warning to be ready for when Jesus comes (especially if it is unexpected and sudden) "don't let him find you asleep" reminds me of a 'message magnet' that used to cling to the metal filing cabinet in the office of a mentor and fellow minister. It had a picture of Jesus approaching from a distance, and the caption read, "Look busy, Jesus is coming." However, this Peter/Mark belief in the impending return of Jesus was subsequently amended in the Gospels that were written after the destruction of the Jerusalem Temple because Jesus had not returned as was expected. But that is a subject for a future exploration!

Mark Chapter 14:
Jesus the Lamb of the Passover

We return now to the analogy of the theatre stage on which two scenes are being acted out simultaneously. On one side of the stage the lights are illuminating Jesus as he talks with his disciples about lessons from the fig tree. On the other side of the stage there is a group made up of chief priests and teachers of the Law, dimly lit but obviously in deep conversation about something. Now Jesus tells of the need to be alert for the end is coming.

Immediately the lights dim on Jesus and his disciples as the scene shifts to a precise "Two days before Passover and the Festival of Thin Bread". The stage lights now blaze upon the parallel plot in which the chief priests and the teachers of the Law of Moses are planning to have Jesus arrested and executed before the Passover and Festival. Again the lights dim on these plotters and shine once again upon Jesus who is now in Bethany and the home of Simon. We leave the analogy of the theatre for a moment.

The early Jesus stories were handed down within the oral tradition of the day and not written until between 30 and 70 years after the execution of Jesus. So keeping in mind the impact of the oral tradition that adapted similar stories in different ways across the developing communities of Christians, I want to consider this episode in Mark and then to explore it further in the other Gospels.

Mark 14:3-9 (New International Version)

3 While he was in Bethany, reclining at the table in the home of Simon the Leper, a woman came with an alabaster jar of very expensive perfume, made of pure nard. She broke the jar and poured the perfume on his head.

4 Some of those present were saying indignantly to one another, "Why this waste of perfume? 5 It could have been sold for more than a year's wages and the money given to the poor." And they rebuked her harshly.

6 "Leave her alone," said Jesus. "Why are you bothering

her? She has done a beautiful thing to me. 7The poor you
will always have with you, and you can help them any time
you want. But you will not always have me. 8She did what
she could. She poured perfume on my body beforehand to
prepare for my burial. 9Truly I tell you, wherever the Gospel
is preached throughout the world, what she has done will
also be told, in memory of her.

Now here is the same story recorded in the Gospel of Matthew some 20 years or so after Mark's version was written.

Matthew 26:6-13 (New International Version)
Jesus Anointed at Bethany
6While Jesus was in Bethany in the home of Simon the Leper,
7a woman came to him with an alabaster jar of very expensive
perfume, which she poured on his head as he was reclining
at the table.
8When the disciples saw this, they were indignant. "Why this
waste?" they asked. 9"This perfume could have been sold at a
high price and the money given to the poor."
10Aware of this, Jesus said to them, "Why are you bothering
this woman? She has done a beautiful thing to me. 11The poor
you will always have with you, but you will not always have
me. 12When she poured this perfume on my body, she did it to
prepare me for burial. 13Truly I tell you, wherever this Gospel
is preached throughout the world, what she has done will
also be told, in memory of her.

Did you notice that there are a couple of minor changes but otherwise Matthew's version is a direct copy of Mark's version? If we are honest in our approach to the Gospels, Mark's narrative was subsequently plagiarized by both Matthew and Luke who added their own corrections and amendments to reflect the needs and experiences of their own communities.

Luke also copied Mark along with a common source with Matthew for the additional stories. This common source is hypothetical but is known by biblical scholars as 'Q': 'quelle' which is German for 'source'. However, Luke appears to have ignored this bottle of expensive perfume story completely and I have to wonder why. Was it something to do with Luke being the gentile outsider who fought long and hard to be accepted as a Jesus follower in his local synagogue where both Jewish and gentile followers of the Jesus Way continued to worship until at least the eighth decade? Perhaps being an outsider was too painful for Luke to include this particular story?

Or was this story as recorded in the other three Gospels about a woman who was or who subsequently became an important insider and central in the work of Jesus, and therefore did not fit neatly into Luke's agenda? Perhaps that woman was Mary Magdalene who was a contemporary of Luke and an important leader of a Christian community?

Or perhaps Luke did not ignore this story after all but, owing to the way in which the Gospel writers selected and placed their stories, simply placed it elsewhere? The Jesus Seminar scholars make the point that the visit to Simon the Pharisee [Luke 7:36-50], possibly in Nain or in Bethany, is the same story. After all it has similar elements:

- A sinful woman who gate-crashed the meal and cried tears that were so great they washed the feet of Jesus that she then proceeded to dry with her hair.

- An expensive bottle of perfume was poured over his feet by this woman.

Luke 7:36-38 (New International Version)
Jesus Anointed by a Sinful Woman
36When one of the Pharisees invited Jesus to have dinner with

him, he went to the Pharisee's house and reclined at the table. [37]A woman in that town who lived a sinful life learned that Jesus was eating at the Pharisee's house, so she came there with an alabaster jar of perfume. [38]As she stood behind him at his feet weeping, she began to wet his feet with her tears. Then she wiped them with her hair, kissed them and poured perfume on them.

And so we now come to the Gospel of John, written at the end of the first century, probably in Ephesus. John's Gospel was very different to the other three. I wonder why John's Gospel has 54 passages that are unique to itself? If these stories concerning Jesus were accurate history, why is it that all three of the earlier Gospels to be written ignored them? There are only 23 passages that appear in John that are also recorded in one or more of the other three Gospels. The major overlaps in the stories appear in the John record of the last week in the life of Jesus.

It therefore seems to me that John either chose to ignore or had little access to the Gospels of Mark, Matthew, Luke or the Q source. Alternatively, it may be that the oral stories concerning Jesus that were told consistently throughout the early Christian church network were only those recording the final week in the life of Jesus. I also conclude that with the additional time for reflecting upon the meaning of the life and death of Jesus, the Gospel of John is much more developed theology concerning Jesus than it is accurate history. Therefore we need to interpret John's Gospel more as theology than history.

Be attentive to the similarities and the differences in the stories.

John 12:1-8 (New International Version)

Jesus Anointed at Bethany

[1]Six days before the Passover, Jesus came to Bethany, where Lazarus lived, whom Jesus had raised from the dead. [2]Here a dinner was given in Jesus' honor. Martha served, while

> Lazarus was among those reclining at the table with him.
> 3Then Mary took about a pint of pure nard, an expensive
> perfume; she poured it on Jesus' feet and wiped his feet with
> her hair. And the house was filled with the fragrance of the
> perfume.
> 4But one of his disciples, Judas Iscariot, who was later to
> betray him, objected, 5"Why wasn't this perfume sold and the
> money given to the poor? It was worth a year's wages." 6He
> did not say this because he cared about the poor but because
> he was a thief; as keeper of the money bag, he used to help
> himself to what was put into it.
> 7"Leave her alone," Jesus replied. "It was intended that she
> should save this perfume for the day of my burial. 8You will
> always have the poor among you, but you will not always
> have me.

So the similarities within the Gospels of Mark, Matthew and John are:

- This incident took place in Bethany.

- An expensive bottle of perfume was broken open.

- There were complaints that the perfume could have been sold and the money given to the poor.

- Jesus defended the woman and her actions.

That's it! Four parts of the story are more or less in agreement across the three Gospels. But for a Bible that some consider to be accurate and without error or contradiction, what can we make of the following differences between John's account and those of Mark and Matthew?

In Mark and Matthew Jesus is in the home of Simon the leper, but in John he is at the home of Lazarus, Mary and Martha.

Although it is obviously nearing the end of the life of Jesus, in Mark and Matthew there is no time placed upon this incident but in John it is precisely placed six days before Passover.

In Mark and Matthew it was a woman who gate-crashed the party and brought with her the expensive perfume, but in John it was Mary, sister of Martha and Lazarus.

In Mark and Matthew the perfume was poured onto the head of Jesus but in John it was poured onto his feet.

In Mark it is some of the guests who complain about the waste of the perfume, but in Matthew it is some of the disciples. However, in John it is Judas Iscariot who complains.

In both Mark and John the perfume could have been sold for more than three hundred silver coins but in Matthew it was an unspecified 'lot of money'.

John alone specifically and uniquely blamed Judas Iscariot and then went on to character assassinate him.

Of course, as unlikely as it may have been, it is just possible that Jesus went first to the home of Simon the leper in Bethany where a woman outsider came and anointed him with perfume, only for Mary to repeat this act when Jesus went to her house. But if it was that way, why did none of the Gospels say so?

Communicating effectively with our contemporary post-modern world

To communicate effectively again with our contemporary post-modern world we will have to be honest about the contradictions within Scripture. We will need to interpret the Bible in a whole new way. The Bible is a powerhouse for personal, corporate and social transformation but it was not written to be read literally.

There now exists a major problem in the narrative: how can Peter/Mark move from the motivation to kill Jesus to the actual opportunity to kill him? They needed a simple device and one that has been used time and again by authors down the centuries:

the deceitful act of a close friend betraying the innocent other. The greatest impact of betrayal upon the listener or reader would not come from one of those who had previously been upset by what Jesus had said or done but from one of the closest.

It is plausible that it could have been the rich young man [Mark 10:17-24] who ran up to Jesus and fell on his knees desperately asking, "I've kept all the Laws of Moses since I was a boy, but there must be something more than this? Tell me what must I do to inherit eternal life!" The last thing that the rich young man wanted to hear was Jesus telling him, "Go and sell everything that you possess and distribute the money to the poor. In that way you will have real treasure in heaven. When you have done all of that, then you can come and follow me."

Mark's narrative then has the young man, doubtless feeling very let down and possibly even smarting with what he personally experienced as a public humiliation by Jesus, walking away very sad because he was not prepared to give up his wealth. The young man had come with a genuine wish to follow Jesus, but the cost was too great. If anyone had a reason to betray Jesus it could have been this spurned young man. But the readers and listeners to the Peter/Mark narrative could have expected such a response from an earnest young man who had felt public humiliation. No, the story needed more than that.

It could have been one of the gentile pig herders or absent pig owners who had their entire lives and businesses destroyed by Jesus when the narrative had him send the legion of evil spirits that indwelt the mad man of Gerasa into the pigs [Mark 5:1-20]. But again the readers and listeners would not have been surprised by an act of revenge for the economic vandalism of Jesus against the swine trade. No, the story needed more than that.

The least surprising would have been a Pharisee who had recently been with Jesus, watching, listening, and waiting: but the story needed more than that. What greater impact could there be than the revulsion of a close friend betraying his Master? And so

Judas Iscariot, who was the keeper of the purse for Jesus and the other disciples, was the one whom Peter/Mark accused of going to the chief priests to trade Jesus for a personally beneficial financial 'payoff' [Mark 14:10-11].

Remembering that both Judas Iscariot and Peter were members of the twelve disciples of Jesus I wonder if there had been a growing jealousy on the part of Judas? After all, it was Peter, James and John who Jesus took with him to climb the mountain of the Transfiguration [Mark 9:2-13]. It was the same three who Jesus took with him further into the Garden of Gethsemane [Mark 14:32-42] immediately before the act of betrayal. Could this jealousy have been exaggerated still further by Jesus publicly bestowing upon Peter the name 'rock'?

Although John's much later Gospel [26:15] states that it was greed that motivated Judas, could the real reason have been, not so much to do with money, but because Judas became increasingly antagonistic toward Jesus owing to his feeling that he was not receiving the recognition that he, as the 'treasurer' of the organization, should have had?

Remember also that Peter had the typical accent of those from Galilee [Mark 14:70]. Indeed the Gospels are specific in indicating that he came from a small fishing village near Capernaum on the Sea of Galilee. Jesus also came from Galilee. Perhaps there was a geo-political element in any rivalry between Judas Iscariot and Simon Peter, and latterly even on the part of Judas towards Jesus?

The name 'Iscariot' is often associated with an identification of a man who originated in the southern Judean town of Kerioth. Bethlehem, David's town, was also in Judea and therefore coupled with the statement that Nathanael made according to John's Gospel [1:46], "Nazareth, can anything good come from there?" may have indicated a pecking order of regional importance in which Judeans looked down upon Galileans, and especially upon those from Nazareth?

I am not suggesting that Judas Iscariot was not the betrayer of Jesus. I have no wish to doubt that the Judas Iscariot betrayal was an actual logos event. As far as I am concerned it could have happened just as Peter/Mark had told the story. But there may have been other reasons for John to single out Judas Iscariot as the betrayer.

Imagine again the analogy of the theatre. The woman has broken the jar of perfume and poured it over Jesus. He has defended her against the accusation of wasting money that could have been given to the poor. Now watch as Judas Iscariot leaves the house of Simon and crosses the stage to talk with the chief priests. The stage lighting dims on Jesus and follows Judas across and then the plotters are once again in full light. But perhaps, for dramatic effect, the lights now glow red as Judas offers to help them arrest Jesus. The plotters are extremely pleased to now have a disciple of Jesus ready to betray him and they offer Judas what amounts to 'blood' money.

Keep the theatre image going. The lights dim once again on the plotters but follow Judas back across the stage and when he arrives we find Jesus and his other disciples already sat around the table in the upper room. A Passover meal is in progress and as Judas enters the room Jesus says that the one who will betray him is now eating with him. Jesus adds:

> 21The Son of Man will go just as it is written about him. But woe to that man who betrays the Son of Man! It would be better for him if he had not been born. [Mark 14:21 (New International Version)]

The eleven other disciples all deny that it will be one of them. Only Judas is silent.

Watch as Jesus takes some bread in his hands and blesses it. He then breaks it and offers it to all twelve sitting around the table. He then takes a cup of wine, blesses it and offers the common cup around the twelve. At the end of this sharing they sing a hymn and Jesus and eleven disciples leave the stage. Judas disappears into the shadows at the back of the stage.

At this point we move away again from the theatre imagery.

Notice that I have not included the words of Jesus:

> [22]While they were eating, Jesus took bread, and when he had given thanks, he broke it and gave it to his disciples, saying, "Take it; this is my body." [23]Then he took a cup, and when he had given thanks, he gave it to them, and they all drank from it. [24]"This is my blood of the covenant, which is poured out for many," he said to them.
> [Mark 14:22-24 (New International Version)]

As far as I understand it, this was a Jewish Passover meal shared among fellow Jews, not the introduction to a new theology or liturgy.

Holy Communion: An invention by Paul?

Linking bread and wine/body and blood was the invention of the Apostle Paul as he struggled to understand the death of Jesus a decade or more after the event. It was Paul who developed and instigated the theology and liturgy of the Lord's Supper. Doubtless he had done so sometime between his first visit to Corinth (50 CE) and when he wrote his first letter to the Corinthians in 54 CE. In between times Paul had visited Ephesus so perhaps it was here that he developed the theology and the liturgy. He included details of these in 1 Corinthians 11:23-25 (New International Version):

> [23] For I received from the Lord what I also passed on to you: The Lord Jesus, on the night he was betrayed, took bread, [24]and when he had given thanks, he broke it and said, "This is my body, which is for you; do this in remembrance of me." [25]In the same way, after supper he took the cup, saying, "This cup is the new covenant in my blood; do this, whenever you drink it, in remembrance of me."

As both Paul and Peter were in Rome at the same time, from the early to the mid-60s CE, I am sure that Paul's theology and liturgy of the Last Supper were made known to Peter and Mark. I also agree with the conclusions of Funk et al in *The Five Gospels* [pages 117-118] when linking Mark's writing with the earlier feeding stories in 6:30-44 (the feeding of the 5000) and 8:1-10 (the feeding of the 4000) to show that the disciples did not understand the theological and liturgical significance of the bread in those stories and still did not realize its significance during that fateful Passover meal: breaking, blessing and distributing.

In the Peter/Mark narrative of the Last Supper the inevitability of what is about to happen is written into the Passover meal: it is a prophecy of the impending death of Jesus written with hindsight and placed into the mouth of Jesus. Having said all that, as far as I am concerned, it matters not that Jesus may not have made the theological or liturgical links between bread and wine/body and blood because each time I am involved in the liturgy of the Last Supper I have no doubt that I experience the sacredness of all in God and God in all.

The Mark narrative now reaches a point where I think that Peter proves himself to be a great man. It is his version of the story of Jesus and so he could have painted himself in the best possible light and airbrushed out unpleasant or unflattering incidents concerning himself. But no, he confesses that he got something else wrong because boastful Peter had responded to Jesus' statement that all his disciples would reject him by declaring that he alone would stand by Jesus. The reply of Jesus was simple and straightforward, stating that by the time dawn broke Peter would have denied Jesus three times [Mark 14:27-31].

As if to rub salt into his own wounded memories Peter tells of his overconfident commitment to Jesus [Mark 14:31]. Peter could have kept this to himself and no one now would be any the wiser. However, out of encouragement to his followers in Rome, Peter was a man big enough to say, "I got it wrong." Here Peter was encouraging his people that they, too, would get things wrong but that was not the end of the matter. In the experiential truth of the death and spiritual resurrection of Jesus, even mistakes become new beginnings.

Was the Garden of Gethsemane a fiction?

Now comes a passage that may be part or all the creation of the writer [Mark 14:32-42]. In the narrative the eleven disciples recognized that Jesus was sad and troubled when he led them to the Garden of Gethsemane. Eight of them were told to sit down while Jesus and the three disciples from his 'inner circle', Peter, James and John, went deeper into the garden to pray. The three heard Jesus say that he was so sad that he felt as if he was dying. Jesus then asked them to remain close by but to be sure to stay awake. Jesus then walked on a little further and knelt down on the ground and prayed.

Up to now it is quite possible that all these have been logos incidents that may have happened just as Peter/Mark told. But now that Jesus was alone and the three had fallen asleep there were no witnesses so no one could have heard Jesus pleading with his Father not to let what seems to be inevitable to actually happen to him. However, in this prayer Peter demonstrated that he knew experientially that Jesus had trusted his Father to be able to do anything. Then Peter also acknowledged that it would have been totally in keeping with the life of Jesus that he was able to resign himself to suffering, if that was to be his Father's will.

Remember that it is Peter, some 30 years after the event, proving once again to be a big man in that he confesses in his telling of the story that he had fallen asleep and failed Jesus, not just once but three times. (Is it significant or just a literary device that Peter's failures often came in sets of three?) But this sleep was not just that which accompanies extreme tiredness. The underlying literary intent is to say that while Jesus was aware of the seriousness and the signs of the immediate time, these disciples still did not understand the gravity of their situation.

When Jesus returned to the three for a third time he woke them again and said that the time had come and that it was now too late to do anything else. The Son of Man was about to be surrendered to sinners – the betrayer had arrived [Mark 14:35-36]. Judas led an armed and common mob, sent by the chief priests, the teachers of the Law of Moses and the Jewish political leaders, right up to Jesus [Mark 14:43-52]. Jesus was betrayed by a kiss.

But why a kiss when all Judas had to do was point at Jesus? As I read this passage I see another literary device: a kiss is an act of close friendship and for the signal to arrest to be such as this just heightens the enormity of the evil contained within a friend's betrayal.
As the mob went to Jesus to tie and bind him, someone among the disciples pulled a sword and swung it at the servant of the high priest and cut off his ear. There is no mention here of an instant example of surgery as Jesus returned the ear to its correct place on the head of the servant [Matthew 26:51].

In the Peter/Mark narrative Jesus calmly asked the people why they had come, carrying weapons, to arrest him. He also reminded them that they could have taken him at any time in recent days while he was teaching in the Temple. And then comes a telltale literary comment of resignation attributed to Jesus, "The Scriptures must be fulfilled." [Mark 14:49 (New International Version)] But I wonder what Scriptures these may be?

Things now happen quickly. First, all his disciples ran away, even though they were supposedly strong and brave. Second, there was a young man who for some unknown reason was wearing just a linen cloth. When the mob grabbed him the young man managed to slip out of the cloth and ran away naked. Who was this young man whom Peter remembered and told about in his memories of the arrest of Jesus? Down the years I have heard mention that this young man was none other than Mark himself, but there is absolutely no proof of such identity.

Also I doubt that there ever was a young naked man in Gethsemane that night. Instead it was Peter/Mark adding 'evidence' of prophetic credibility and authenticity to this part of the Jesus story by referencing Amos 2:16, "Even the bravest warriors will flee naked on that day," declares the LORD. (New International Version) The brave and the strong, along with this naked young man, all running away was a literary device, not to record an actual historical logos event but to show the fulfillment of the Amos prophecy.

Peter's denial

The drama continues and I have no reason to doubt that these following events actually happened. Imagine again that you are in the theater and you watch as Jesus is dragged across the open stage and thrown on the floor at the feet of the high priest. The chief priests and the teachers of the Law of Moses surround him. It hurts as you watch, almost intruding upon a scene of immense pain following the betrayal by a close friend and the desertion by the rest of the disciples.

A crowd gathers to watch and to listen. And then in the shadows you see Peter creep into the courtyard and sit down among the guards. It is cold and he warms himself in front of the fire. You listen as the high priest and his cohort try to find someone who will testify against Jesus so that he can be taken to Pilate and the death sentence requested.

Listen as the people in the crowd offer supposed 'eye witness' reports that they had heard Jesus threaten to destroy the Temple and to rebuild it in three days. But they cannot agree and fierce arguments break out.

Finally the high priest asks Jesus directly why he is silent and saying nothing in his own defense. Jesus refuses to respond so the high priest asks him if he thinks that he is the Messiah, the Son of God.

This time you hear Jesus say, "I am," said Jesus. "And you will see the Son of Man sitting at the right hand of the Mighty One and coming on the clouds of heaven." [Mark 14:62 (New International Version)]

This is all too much and you continue to watch as the high priest flies into a rage, ripping his own cloak and shouting to the crowd, "Why do we need any more witnesses?" he asked. [64]"You have heard the blasphemy. What do you think?" They all condemned him as worthy of death. [Mark 14:63-64 (New International Version)]

As you watch you have a growing sense of revulsion as the crowd begins to randomly chant until there is just one loud shout of unison, "Put him to death! Put him to death!"

You want to protect this innocent man from further torment but you sit there watching helplessly as the crowd begins to spit on Jesus. He is roughly blindfolded and fists rain down upon him. Then the guards get up from the warmth of the fire and push their way through the crowd. Just when you think that they are going to protect Jesus, they push back the onlookers and then start beating him themselves.

Now the lights go down on that part of the stage and your attention is taken away from the confusion and the physical assault on Jesus. Once again you are looking to the fire where Peter has been watching and listening at a distance. One of the high priest's servant girls turns and notices Peter and then shouts, "I recognize you! You are one of the friends of this Jesus! You and he are both from Galilee!"

She draws the attention of the crowd away from Jesus and onto Peter. You do not want to hear Peter's reply. It is all too much for you, but his reply comes loud and clear, "You are mistaken. I don't know the man!"

Above the commotion you hear the sound of the crowing of a rooster.

But the servant girl persists and follows Peter as he attempts to escape the stage, "This man is one of the friends of Jesus! Look, he dresses and he sounds like a Galilean!"

"I tell you that you are mistaken!"

She does not let go, "You are a liar. You know that you are one of them!"

Peter replies immediately, "I swear by all that is holy that I do not know that man!"

Above the commotion you hear the sound of the crowing of a rooster a second time.

Peter hears it as well and drops to his knees in floods of tears, remembering that Jesus had told him that he would deny Jesus three times before the rooster crowed a second time [Mark 14:66-72].

The stage goes to blackout.

Peter/Mark have captured what I am convinced were logos events concerning the priestly trial of Jesus. I have no doubt that Peter was there in the courtyard denying his close friend and leader, Jesus of Nazareth.

Mark Chapters 15 and 16:
The trial and execution of Jesus

According to the narrative [Mark 15:1-5], the accusers, those with religious and local political power, then dragged Jesus before Pilate. The Roman Governor, having listened to the accusations then turned to Jesus and asked him if he thought that he was the king of the Jews?

If Jesus answered 'yes' then it was a foregone conclusion: there was no king but the one (Herod) who had been appointed by Caesar. A 'yes' would have led immediately to crucifixion.

Jesus simply replied that he was not saying such a thing but his accusers and Pilate himself had said so. As the accusers came back with more outrageous claims against Jesus, Pilate noticed that Jesus listened in silence. So Pilate again asked Jesus if he wanted to defend himself but Jesus amazed Pilate by keeping silent.

Barabbas – another fictional character?

In my opinion, what then follows in the narrative becomes more mythos than logos [Mark 15:6-15]. Although it may seem far-fetched as far as most Christians are concerned, I doubt even the existence of Barabbas as a real person. As far as my research informs me there never was a Roman custom of releasing a prisoner at the Passover festival. The four Gospels all explain Barabbas as something slightly different: Mark calls him a 'prisoner'; Matthew a 'well-known terrorist'; Luke a 'rioter'; John a 'terrorist'. He may have been all of these things, but why should a Roman Governor, as unpleasant as Pilate is said to have been, offer to set free a terrorist in exchange for this poor, innocent man from Nazareth?

Think about his name, 'bar-Abbas': it means 'son of the father'. How coincidental is that? So here in this story of choices we have the people offered the choice between Jesus, known as the 'Son of the Father', and Barabbas, also known as 'son of the father'. As I see this story of choices I think that I can detect something of Peter's developing theology coming through. Like the crowd before Pilate, we all have a personal choice to make about the way in which we live our lives. Within us all is both the 'Son of the Father' and the 'son of the father'. Choose the former, the Jesus Way, and we commit ourselves to living by the values of the Kingdom, putting others first as we serve those in need. Choose the latter and we are choosing to live our lives in our way, self before others, and expecting to be served rather more than we choose to serve.

If we choose the Jesus Way, the way of the 'Son of the Father', then Peter's theology reminds us that we are reassured by the Jesus Spirit that we are walking in the ways of God. Sharing in his passion will be evidenced in our lives as we live the servant ways of Christ. And from his own bitter experience of denial and failure, Peter can now encourage his listeners and readers to remain faithful to God in Jesus.

Although when it really mattered in Gethsemane before the mob and in the courtyard before the chief priests, Peter had made his choice to follow the 'son of the father', now, even in the grip of persecution, Peter can honestly proclaim that his choice is to follow the 'Son of the Father'. This is wonderful evidence of the spiritual liberation and renewal of Peter!

Pilate then ordered his soldiers to scourge Jesus with their whips and then to execute him on a cross. As they exited into the courtyard the soldiers called the rest of the troops to join them in mocking Jesus. They stripped Jesus and put a purple robe on him, the symbol of being a king. They then made a crown of thorns and roughly pushed it onto his head. They gave him a stick, a symbol of the king's scepter. They then beat him with the stick, spat on him and then fell on their knees before him pretending to worship him. When they had finished their fun they removed the purple cloak and put his own miserable clothes back on him. They led him away to his execution.

The execution of Jesus is dealt with in more detail in *Setting Jesus Free* [pages 158-166] so suffice it now just to say that it must have been an awfulness that was even too great for words to describe. Indeed it appeared to be so difficult to depict that the Gospel accounts are, in places, contradictory leading me to increasingly wonder what really happened to the body of Jesus after the crucifixion.

According to Peter/Mark a highly respected member of the Jewish council, Joseph from Arimathea, overcame his fear of punishment by being associated with a crucified victim and went to Pilate to request the body of Jesus. Surprised that Jesus had died so quickly, Pilate called for confirmation. As soon as the officer said that Jesus was dead Pilate released the body into the care of Joseph. Jesus was taken down from the cross and wrapped in a linen shroud. Joseph took the dead body to a newly carved tomb and laid Jesus in there. He then rolled a large stone across the entrance. The narrative explains that Mary Magdalene and Mary the mother of Joseph (Arimathea perhaps?) watched this happening and so knew where the body had been placed [Mark 15:42-47].

What really happened to the body of Jesus?

Crossan, in his book *Jesus: A Revolutionary Biography*, makes a very plausible case that the body of Jesus went the way of all crucified – it was left on the cross for vultures to tear apart and eat, and for wild dogs beneath to wait for the scraps to fall from the pecking at the dead flesh. Crossan quotes from the writings of Josephus who reported on:

• The Syrian Governor Publius Quinctilius Varus crucifying 2000 Jewish rebels in the rebellion that followed the death, in 4 BCE of Herod the Great.

• The Roman Governor Florus, in 66 CE, crucified 3600 citizens of Jerusalem, including women and children.

• The army of Titus, in 70 CE, entered Jerusalem and crucified an unknown number of its citizens although Josephus estimates as many as 500 a day all nailed to crosses along the walls of the city.

Crossan also cites Martin Hengel (1977) whose book reported on various authors of the first century concerning what they said about crucifixion. Hengel concludes that those who were crucified were nailed to the cross and, after death, left hanging there as food for vultures and scraps for wild dogs waiting beneath.

Christianity is certain that it needs a physically resurrected Jesus as clearly and unambiguously stated in its creeds and doctrines. However, many followers of the Jesus Way are now content with a spiritual resurrection so that a bodily raised Jesus is irrelevant to our discipleship.

And so we arrive at the climax of the Peter / Mark narrative. It has been a wonderful creative story, a biography of the life and death of Jesus. And here comes the golden thread of the entire narrative being made explicit in the experiences of the followers of Jesus, captured in the empty tomb [Mark 16:1-8]: "Jesus will be found among the living, not among the dead!"

Since my book *Setting Jesus Free* was published I have been asked many times, "Well, do you believe in the resurrection of Jesus? Yes or no?"

My answer is like that of the many politicians who all compete for our votes come an election. My answer is, "Well, it's both 'yes' and 'no'!"

This response is often followed up with a supplementary question that goes something like, "But the creeds of the church tell us that Jesus was physically raised from the dead, so, do you believe in a physical resurrection of Jesus?"
My answer is: "No, I don't."

The conversation often then progresses to the next supplementary, more of an accusation than a question: "Then what do you believe?"

My response is always, "I believe, most emphatically, in the spiritual resurrection of Jesus! As I understand these things, without the spiritual resurrection of Jesus there is no hope for the future for us or for this world. It is the Namaskaram/Namaste Spirit that indwells all people. The Eternal Spirit (God) is like a river that has no beginning and no end. It flows continually. At a given point we are each created as mind and body, the 'hat' and 'coat' of the Eternal Spirit. The day comes when the hat and coat are no longer necessary and are cast away. But the Eternal Spirit that is the Alpha and the Omega, but without beginning and without end, continues to flow. Jesus lives because the Eternal Spirit lives."

I take this line because this Eternal Spirit does not require assent to 4th century creeds and doctrines that are increasingly detrimental to the life and witness of both the Church and the Jesus Spirit in ordinary lives today. This spiritual 'resurrection' of Jesus involves a commitment to living those values that are found within the Christian Testament stories: values that bear witness to the life and death of Jesus within the Eternal Spirit. As far as I am concerned, this spiritual 'resurrection' of Jesus is not about having to believe a set of explanatory words that satisfied the 4th century Church Councils but no longer make sense to the majority of people in this country today.

An email was sent to me in the lead up to Easter 2010 by a reader of the sermons on my website. Although I have taken poetic license and edited his email, he summed up where I am in the following words: "The point is to be Jesus, not just a follower or believer in, but to walk in his shoes. Whether the stories are true isn't the point. The point is to learn from the parables, myths and stories to help you to lead a better, more fulfilled, caring and socially motivated and connected life and to feel closer to whatever is the mysterious energy that we call god."

In my opinion the Church in the industrialized world will only survive if its people genuinely live the values of the compassion, servant-hood and unconditional love that are the Kingdom – the Jesus Way. The Church has no future if it bases membership upon outmoded creeds and doctrines that are contrary to scientific advances, Darwinism, sociology, psychology and so on.

As I was writing this chapter in March 2010 I was, as always, keeping a watchful eye on the newspapers and news broadcasts because a spirituality that is not grounded within the realities of daily blood, sweat and tears is a spirituality that is not worth having.

My 2010 Easter Sunday morning sermon started by saying that I did not want to be a discouragement to the listeners but it commenced in the dirt and grime that is life for many people. As followers of Jesus living in the real world, I asked what we really had to celebrate. I referenced the dwindling church congregations across this country, recent newspaper stories and television news broadcasts, and stated that it is so easy to lose heart when we cannot see light at the end of the tunnel.

In the week leading up to Easter in 2010 we had watched the horrendous events following the suicide bomb attacks on the Moscow Metro; elsewhere, in the Russian republic of Dagestan, at least nine people were killed by two bombs; in London thirteen youths were accused of murdering a 15-year-old boy at Victoria Underground station; more peacekeepers in Afghanistan were killed or seriously injured; Israeli war planes bombed the Gaza Strip, following the killing of two Israeli soldiers; 25 people were shot dead in an attack on a Sunni village south of Baghdad; the white supremacist Eugene Terreblanche was murdered in South Africa; and so it went on.

And over the long months of that past winter conversation about the awful weather had never been far from our lips. I reminded the congregation that although there is conflicting evidence concerning global climate change I align myself with those who live on the side of caution. If climate is changing because humankind is being profligate with its carbon footprint then I need to take action to reduce my contribution to the long-term damage to the ecosystems of this world. This eco damage is already hitting the poorest and most vulnerable long before it will really impact adversely upon we who are the primary causes of the climate changes.

On Good Friday 2010, I received an email from a trustworthy friend who leads a small Christian charity in Uganda. This is what he said: "Last month there was a serious landslide in Bududa, a district neighboring Mbale. Heavy rains caused devastation as hundreds of people lost everything, and sadly for many that included their lives. In the main parish involved, only 7 out of 365 people survived. With continuing rains the authorities have evacuated the area, forcing some 3000 people into a temporary camp."

Yet, both Australia and Cyprus had been in the grip of their worst droughts in a century. We continue to watch television coverage of melting ice flows, and the devastation caused by high winds and forest fires. In Britain, as well as in much of Europe, that past winter was longer and colder than over recent years.

However, perhaps not all the bad weather is attributable to global climate change? Even when we thought that spring had arrived, Scotland and Northern Ireland were plunged back into some of the worst blizzards of the winter resulting in a tragic bus crash and the death of a 17-year-old girl in South Lanarkshire.

That winter also saw record snowfall, nicknamed 'snowmageddon', on the east coast of the USA. Those who watched the spectacular Winter Olympics will remember that the Canadians had to carry snow by the lorry load to enable the games to proceed. But the weather experts tell us that this was the result, not of global climate change, but the impact of El Niño, the warm current of water that flows east toward South America.

When we look at the television news it is all too easy to despair and feel that it is all but over for the human race. Depressing isn't it?

The ongoing truth of the Jesus experience

Nevertheless, in spite of the evidence all around us, it is the truth of the ongoing presence of the Eternal Spirit, explained by open and progressive Christians as the spiritual resurrection of Jesus, that gives me hope for the present and for the future. Light will always overcome the darkness of this world. And so, just for a short time I reminded the congregation yet again of the different Gospel accounts of what happened that first Easter weekend. The disciples of Jesus, both women and men, were in deep despair. The hopes that they had built up over the previous three years or so had come to an end with Jesus of Nazareth executed on a cross. Such crucifixion was the Roman punishment for rebels, traitors and troublemakers. Although it is contradicted in the other Gospels, in Matthew's account it was Mary Magdalene and the other Mary who went to the tomb expecting to find the dead among the dead. However, in the stories and experiences of the followers of Jesus, they found what they had not expected, that the stone that had covered the tomb had been rolled away. Whether or not the events of that Easter morning, as recorded in the conflicting Gospel accounts, actually happened as written really does not bother me. Not all the Gospel descriptions can be right because they name different people going to the tomb and very different events occurring when they arrived there.

For those who believe that Jesus was physically raised from the dead, then that is correct for you because it is your experience of the sacred met in Jesus. However, there are other followers of Jesus whose understanding and experience of the Easter stories does not depend upon a physically raised Jesus. For me it does not matter, because either way the Eternal Truth is in my experience of the narrative's reassurance of the angel that Jesus was not in the tomb because God had raised him to life!

Between 30 and 70 years after that first Easter, the persecuted and oppressed Gospel writers were trying to articulate their experiences that Jesus had become the breaker of the final barrier, death itself. The glorious truth of the Easter message is that life is always greater than death; that hope is always greater than fear and despair.

Many will have experienced at some time the traditional Maundy (Holy) Thursday evening service in which lights are extinguished and people leave the church in darkness, symbolic of the light of Christ overcome by the darkness of death. But this has been for a short time because on Easter Sunday morning we rejoice that light and hope have triumphed yet again over the darkness of dull despair! Light will always overcome darkness.

It is in that Easter message where I find the constant hope to face the uncertainties of that which is yet to come, including those that are economic and financial: violence and war; environmental degradation and climate change. It is my personal experience of the presence of the spiritually risen Jesus that gives me the hope that love and compassionate, sacrificial servant-hood will always overcome injustice and hatred.

But we must not sit back and let God do the work for us. Too often we wait for God to act when God is waiting for us to get involved. The Jesus Spirit challenges us to live the concerns and values of the Kingdom so that our children and our children's children will have a future worth looking towards with confidence and joy.

You and I are accountable for living the Easter message today and every day. The resurrection of Jesus is not just about something that happened 2000 years ago. Nor, as I understand these things, is resurrection about something that will happen in the future. Resurrection is a daily occurrence in all of our lives reminding us that there is more to this life than the hardships that we suffer from time to time.

The Eternal Truth of the 'resurrection' of Jesus reminds us of the hope that we have that no matter how unpleasant and challenging life may be at any one time, there is more to this life than hopelessness. No matter how demanding may be our economic, political, religious and social pressures we can live the resurrection story so that darkness will always give way to light. By the way in which the Kingdom values of perfect love, compassion and servant-hood operate, even that which appears to be hopeless and full of darkness are, in reality, new beginnings.

Living daily the Easter story

West offers a similar illustration of what it means to live daily the Easter story. He says that whenever a prejudice is surrendered then that is a death within the person concerned. West goes onto say that to discover to die in this way is to become skilled in how to live. To live the Easter story in this way is a constant second-birthing into an advanced degree of wisdom and experience [2008, pages 26-27].

Also we need to remember that nowhere in the Gospels did Jesus say, "One day I will be the resurrection and the life." Only John's Gospel has Jesus saying anything like this when Jesus was talking to Martha, the sister of Mary and Lazarus: he said, "I am the resurrection and the life. He who believes in me will live, even though he dies."

Please notice that when Jesus spoke of the resurrection and the life he did not speak of a time to come. "I am the resurrection and the life" is present tense – it is now. It is to be encountered and lived this moment by each one of us. From time to time life will seem to take a turn for the worse, but when it does do not let go of the Eternal Truth of the Easter stories: Jesus is the resurrection and the life in our here and now. The Jesus Spirit is not consigned to history among the dead. The Jesus Spirit is among the living, where you and I live our lives.

Being followers of the Jesus Way indwelt with the Jesus Spirit is to live the resurrection life here and now. To do so will enable us to experience the fullness of life, no matter what happens to us day by day. The resurrection life is also the abundant life, no matter what our anxieties, doubts, failures and regrets may be. It is the life of overflowing peace within our uncertainties and distress. To experience the resurrection life is to experience God indwelling us in the present.

In my experience the truth of the empty tomb is that the Jesus Spirit is not found among the dead but is always here among us, we who are the living. The resurrection of Jesus is always about the present. It is the sacred invitation to us to live the values of the Kingdom in which we are constantly dying to our selfishness and greed, so that we may live. It is in this that we will be able to proclaim the great and joyful Easter chant, "In my life, in this moment, among these people, Christ is risen: Alleluia!"

Appendices

Appendix One

Recently I re-discovered John Powell's wonderful little book *Fully Human Fully Alive*. One sentence stood out like a mountain peak above a dusty and barren landscape when he suggested that each of our personal worlds is as big as our hearts. The book was given me many years ago by a man who subsequently spent time in prison for offences against children. Whenever I see the spine of that book on my bookshelf I am reminded of the evil that can be deep inside the most respectable and loving of people. The injuries that he did to innocent children will remain with them far longer than was his relatively short imprisonment. But they and he are still sacred and anger that is bottled up, or the seeking of revenge, or the inability to forgive actually kills the one who holds the anger or seeks the revenge or finds it impossible to forgive. In the end, perfect love drives out fear of the past, the present and the future. Dr. Jim Swire who lost his daughter Flora in the Lockerbie disaster is an amazing example of this principle at work. However, I am convinced that all people are capable of loving more than themselves.

Appendix Two

Hans Küng

Küng's *Christianity: The Religious Situation of Our Time* was published in 1994 with an English translation a year later. I remember trying to read it when it first appeared in English but I found it difficult to understand and promptly placed it onto a bookshelf "just in case it comes in handy one day!" I was obviously not ready for it in 1995 but in 2010 its re-reading has opened my understanding to a host of new issues. The foundations for Küng's book are stated clearly even before his title page:

- No peace among the nations without peace among the

religions.

• No peace among the religions without dialogue between the religions.

• No dialogue between the religions without investigation of the foundations of the religions.

In this Küng was a forerunner of Karen Armstrong and her involvement in the Charter for Compassion. Küng's is a brilliant book that not only spoke clearly to the Church in 1995 but it continues to speak just as much 15 years later. The difference is that I was not ready for it then but was stimulated and invigorated by it upon a second, much later reading. Surely that is the point of theology; Church, creeds, doctrines and personal experiences – there can be no standing still. It is not wrong to progress in thinking even if that means a complete about turn from one understanding to an opposite.

One of the major points that struck me forcefully, second time around, is Küng's assertion that the history of Christianity has been one of "a quite arbitrary and contradictory sequence of contrasting ideas or events which are held together by nothing and nobody? Or is there more?"

His answer is that the one thread that can hold together creeds, doctrines, literalism, fundamentalism, liberalism, Catholicism, Protestantism, and so on is none of these descriptors but by the person of Jesus of Nazareth. It is back to that authentic Jesus and his uniting and reformist wisdom message that I am attempting, as best that I can, to travel. It is indeed a quest that requires going backwards before we can progress forwards with a Jesus message that is truly relevant to today. It is to this man, Jesus of Nazareth, that I look rather than to the later explanatory fictions of the creeds and doctrines of 4th century Christianity. Whether or not that makes me a heretic, others must judge.

But let me define the word 'heretic'. According to the Chambers 21st Century Dictionary "a 'heretic' is someone who has views and opinions that conflict with those of the majority." This is often the case but I would wish to add that the heretic could also be one who has the support of many, perhaps most of the 'silent majority', but lacks the support of the outspoken and powerful elite.

Now let me define what constitutes being a 'prophet'. Although I would take issue with some of the parts of the definition, according to the Chambers 21st Century Dictionary "a 'prophet' is someone who is able to express the will of God or a god, for example, in the Bible any of the writers of prophecy in the Old Testament; and in Islam, the Prophet Muhammad."

Chambers also defines a prophet as someone "who claims to be able to tell what will happen in the future" recognizing, perhaps, that there are the magicians and crystal ball gazers who have nothing of importance to say except to the vulnerable. On the other hand there are those who should be listened to: individuals such as British scientist James Lovelock who worked mainly in Britain but for some years also in Houston and Pasadena, and Americans such as Al Gore and Sen. Joe Lieberman. There are campaigning organizations on both sides of the Atlantic including Christian Aid, Oxfam, Operation Noah, Greenpeace, Friends of the Earth, the Evangelical Climate Initiative, Toronto Climate Campaign Group, and many more. All are warning of the impact of climate change and global warming on the poorest first, and then upon the rest of us.

Appendix Three

Additional relevant background information

Matthew's community

This may, eventually, have been situated in one of a number of places including Antioch, Judea and the Decapolis, but there are so many maritime references that my personal choice is Caesarea Maritima. Matthew's Gospel tends to be more Jewish Christian than gentile

Christian in its theological development; its view of Messianic history; its developing theology of God and Jesus. It should be read with full recognition that it is written within a particular social context and offers a particular social commentary.

Dr. Tzvee Zahavy, a professor and rabbi who is an acknowledged expert in Judaism, Hebrew, Jewish and Religious Studies has written on the Judaism of the Mishnaic period, including references to the Yavneh rabbinic academy. This was set up southwest of Jerusalem after a number of rabbis and followers had been allowed to escape the Roman assault on Jerusalem. Following the Judaism of Rabbi Hillel, they settled and remained at Yavneh from around 75 to 90. During the first century CE there was not one but many forms of Judaism. Matthew's community may have been one of the Jewish Christian sects that had some association with Yavneh. However, it continued to develop its Judeo-Christian theology to increasing opposition from the Yavneh rabbinic academy. In 80 CE the rabbis of Yavneh decreed that Jewish followers of the Jesus Way were no longer welcome and Matthew's community was excluded.

It is this exclusion and therefore denial of their birthright as Jews that led to the bitter polemic of Matthew's Gospel against the Pharisees and Sadducees. The Gospel of Matthew was written in the context of an appalling Jewish family quarrel. Therefore all the 'let his blood be upon our heads and upon our children's children' etc, that has led to appalling treatment of Jews by Christians ever since that time, was probably words of condemnation placed by Matthew's community into the mouths of Pharisees and Sadducees as representatives of the Yavneh Rabbinic Academy. Therefore, such an event of 'let his blood' etc before Pilate possibly never happened.

Had later Christians understood the polemic of the family feud of Matthew and Yavneh, anti-Semitism may never have become a problem and may never had reached its height of brutality with the Nazi Holocaust.

None of this is exact science and most of it, as with both mythos interpretations of logos history, is speculation.

Luke's mythos and logos

When reading the mythos and logos within Luke's Gospel it is vitally important that we understand both the social context of the time and the personalities involved, otherwise we will fail to comprehend the reality of what Luke was trying to communicate.

Luke was probably a Greek-speaking non-Jew, a Syrian from Antioch. I am of the opinion that Luke was a Paul convert, well-schooled in Paul's version of Judaism. He travelled with Paul to the Jerusalem Conference in 50 CE as Paul's proof that gentiles did not need to become Jews before they could be followers of the Jesus Way. This is the social context of Luke, the outsider trying to get in and to be accepted by the leaders of the Jerusalem Church.

Luke's Gospel was written in Greek, with Greek rather than Jewish philosophical understandings. It followed the disastrous uprising by Jews against the Roman occupation army. It was, therefore, a social commentary on the Jewish longing for Yahweh to deliver them from their Roman oppressors. But it also reflected Luke's own situation as an oppressed Greek within the Roman Empire sharing in a similar way that which Jews were suffering.

It was within this context that Luke conveyed his developing mythos concerning Jesus. Although I doubt that Mary ever said the Magnificat, it is a theology reflecting a commentary of the socio-political situation of the time. Luke's Jewish Christian and gentile Christian community in Antioch was suffering as a result of being in a land occupied by the all-conquering power of Rome. But here is political hope for the people because, according to Luke, it was in Jesus the Christ that God came to turn the world the right way up, and although Rome had executed him, that was not the end. The day would come when God would bring down the powerful and the proud. When that day came the poor and oppressed, such as them, would again be free.

In the meantime Luke was also commenting on the development

of love in the Christian church where all things were held in common, and, as a result of Paul's teaching, there was no separation in Christ between male and female; Jew and Greek; master and slave – at least within the Christian community. This was Luke's social commentary that while the Romans and their Jewish collaborators seemed to enjoy the selfish fruits of power and domination, the followers of the Jesus Way were supporting one another by feeding the hungry, clothing the poor, healing the sick and setting slaves free. Luke was contrasting the selfishness of Empire with the Agape love of God and the living proclamation of God's Kingdom on earth there and then.

The three Gospels that followed after Mark contain a more developed mythos theology as their communities attempted to explain their ongoing experiences of what they believed was the sacred presence of the Jesus Spirit long after that first Easter. Both Matthew and Luke were adding mythos stories to Mark's Gospel. This was to answer questions that were arising as a later generation of Jesus Way followers tried to interpret and understand their Jesus experiences and stories for themselves.

Doubtless there were questions concerning how Matthew or Luke could say that, in their experiences, Jesus was the Son of God. The answer that Matthew came up with, and then copied by Luke, is contained both in the genealogy of Jesus and the Virgin Birth story. Note, however, that the Matthew and Luke genealogies are different as are their birth stories of Jesus. Both cannot be right, but that is how mythos theology developed because they were written expressions that attempted to describe the indescribable experiences of the sacred.

Appendix Four
The Letters of Paul

Christians generally accept the major influence of the Apostle Paul concerning the establishing and maintenance of early communities of followers of the Jesus Way. But often we do not comprehend the extent of that influence. However, it is not quite that simple! I have many books and commentaries concerning the Christian Testament, including analysis of the Epistles, and I openly acknowledge that there is no universal agreement on the locations and dates of the writing of the various letters of Paul. Nor is there universal agreement on which of the letters attributed to Paul are genuinely written by him and those that were written subsequent to his execution. None of this can ever be an exact science and therefore it should be of no surprise that there is both controversy and debate between biblical scholars.

For example, Crossan (2007) points out that there are 13 letters attributed to Paul in the Christian Testament and, along with the parts of the Book of Acts that are about Paul, this Apostle commands half the entire Christian Testament. In my studies I rely upon *The New Jerome Biblical Commentary* (1989) more than any other commentary, mainly because I find that it is thoroughly researched by its contributors and offers a fair consensus among all those that sit on my bookshelves. For brevity at this point I am following the details contained in that commentary concerning the seven that were authentic Paul. The authors of the source articles in *The New Jerome Biblical Commentary* are shown in brackets:

- 1 Thessalonians, written in 50 CE in Corinth to the church community in Thessalonica [Collins, Raymond, F.]
- 1 Corinthians, written in the spring of 54 CE in Ephesus to the church community in Corinth [Murphy-O'Connor, Jerome, OP]
- Galatians, written later in 54 CE again in Ephesus to the church community in Galatia [Fitzmyer, Joseph, SJ]
- Philippians, written originally as three separate manuscripts when Paul was travelling sometime after 54 CE and completed after he was released from imprisonment in Caesarea between 57-58 CE to the church community in Philippi [Byrne, Brendan, SJ]

- 2 Corinthians, written originally as two to five separate manuscripts in the spring and summer of 55 CE from different towns in Macedonia and Illyricum, to the church communities in Corinth and Achaia [Murphy-O'Connor, Jerome, OP]
- Romans, written in 57 or 58 CE in Corinth to the church community in Rome [Fitzmyer, Joseph, SJ]
- Philemon, written between 61 and 63 CE when Paul was under house arrest in Rome to the church community in Colossae [Fitzmyer, Joseph, SJ]

Crossan (2007) suggests that others were probably written after Paul's death to water down Paul's radicalism. Even though written as though by Paul, on close inspection they are actually anti-Pauline on slavery and patriarchy. Crossan continues by stating that the later letters progressively take Paul from radical through liberal into a conservative reactionary theology.

In exploring Crossan's three probably not authentic letters I continue to reference *The New Jerome Biblical Commentary*:

- 2 Thessalonians written between 51 and 100 CE using 1 Thessalonians as a very close guide, but location of writing is too suspect to draw any conclusions [Giblin, Charles, SJ]
- Colossians, written between 70 and 80 CE, possibly written in Ephesus [Horgan, Maurya]
- Ephesians written between 70 and 80 CE, by someone who was well schooled in Pauline literature, but location of writing is too suspect to draw any conclusions [Kobelski, Paul]

Also according to Crossan the three certainly not authentic letters are 1 Timothy, 2 Timothy and Titus. These were all probably written around 100 C.E. in Ephesus [Wild, Robert, S.J.]

Appendix Five

John's social context and commentary

John's Gospel was probably written by the followers of the teaching of John the Beloved Disciple and was also set within the context of Jewish Christian expulsion from synagogues and continuing oppression of Rome. It should be noted, however, that there is some argument that the Beloved Disciple was, in fact, a Gnostic leader, Mary Magdalene [Mary the Great]. Right from its time of writing, the Gnostic sects of followers of the Jesus Way treated John's Gospel with great respect. The Gnostics believed that God is discovered through experience, knowledge and reason rather than through a set of 'orthodox' teachings, many of which were later developed into 4th century creedal beliefs and church dogma. The Gnostics had beliefs but they did not insist that they had all the truth and nothing but the truth.

Whereas orthodox Christianity, in common with the Romans and Greeks, pronounced a God 'out there', the Gnostics believed that God was within and could be discovered by knowing themselves. As a consequence of the Gnostic support, other followers of the Jesus Way who rejected the Gnostic interpretation of the life and death of Jesus marginalized the Gospel of John. It almost did not make it into the Christian Testament because it is at odds with the Gospels of Matthew and Luke, and to a lesser extent that of Mark.

But there was a further social context and commentary for John's community in Ephesus. John's Gospel was written some 5 to 15 years after Luke's Gospel. It reflected the context of the followers of John's teaching and church leadership now moved out of Jerusalem after disagreements with the followers of Peter and Paul who had developed a hierarchy of bishops, pastors and teachers and so on. John's community continued to develop John the Beloved Disciple's understanding of Jesus as the Good Shepherd – a metaphor found nowhere else in the Gospels.

So whereas Peter and Paul operated managerial 'command

and control' top down leadership styles for their followers, John introduced the servant shepherd model in which the leaders were to serve rather than to be served and to gently guide rather than to tell and to command. Both Peter's and Paul's management model reflected the control of Roman Imperialism whereas John's management style was contrary to the norm.

Careful reading of the Gospel of John needs to be within the context also of the three Letters attributed to John. The social context here was that of suspicion and rivalry with other Christian communities, especially those who followed either the teaching of the Apostle Peter or, more likely, that of Mary Magdalene's Gnostic community. However, both these assertions can be challenged. In Peter's case because John's Gospel draws in part upon Peter's interpreted experiences recorded in Mark's Gospel, and in Magdalene's case because she was very much revered among the Gnostics and John's Gospel was considered by many 'mainstream' Christian leaders at the time of its writing as being too Gnostic. This is certainly an area for further investigation:

1 John is concerned with overcoming the world by following God's way of loving others, although there is the command to be aware of the anti-Christ who would lead followers astray.

2 John is an exhortation to remain faithful and to offer missionary hospitality to those of John's community, but also to avoid and to take action against the dissidents who rejected the idea that Jesus was God in the flesh. 2 John also mentions care to be taken when confronting 'the elect lady'. This could have been a simple reference to 'another church' or it could have been a warning reflecting a growing disagreement with the 'the elect lady' being the other important Christian community in Ephesus at that time, that which followed the teaching of Mary Magdalene.

3 John is an attack upon Diotrephes, who had broken away from

John's community and then excommunicated any of his followers who offered sacred hospitality to members of John's community. It also praises Gaius for offering hospitality.

Appendix Six

Applying agape love today

That year is also this year. The Lord's favor– agape love and acceptance – then is the same message of God's agape love towards each one of us now, regardless of who or what we are. It should be a salutary warning to us and to the Church in this time that our power and influence is not in knowing and speaking words of wisdom alone but it is in doing something about those words in practical daily living and in challenging the social injustices of our time.

It is about doing whatever we can to eradicate unnecessary and avoidable poverty. It is about having time to care for our friends, family and neighbors when they fall upon the hard times of ill health, age, redundancy, bereavement, or even of being imprisoned for some misdemeanor. It is about accepting that there are many gateways to the God-experience, and that as followers of the Jesus Way we welcome, respect, accept and encourage all those who have found alternative gateways to that of Jesus of Nazareth.

It means getting involved in and encouraging interfaith understanding and activity. It is about ensuring that our individual and corporate carbon footprints are made as small as possible so that we do not steal our children's futures. It is about ensuring that female and male have equal opportunities within the Church just as within society. It is about accepting that the Love that is God can be found and expressed in committed heterosexual as well as in committed single sex relationships. It is about supporting attempts to redress the economic imbalances and evils that keep us the minority in luxury, while the majorities are denied even the basic rights of clean water, good health and education.

It may sound as though I am preaching a message of despair when I say that, apart from the ex-colonial parts of Africa such as Nigeria and Uganda, the 'traditional' or 'established' churches in Europe and the English-speaking world are dying. It is far too simplistic an argument on my part, but from my pastoral experiences I suggest that these churches are fading owing to two major yet opposite points:

In some local church communities the messages and wisdom offered seem so often to be little more than irrelevant and outdated ideas and non-challenging platitudes. I put into this category the type of preaching that is little more than 'let us be kind to animals'. I am not suggesting that it is not important to be kind to all creation, far from it, but there are far more important issues to be addressed by those who seek to follow a relevant life-changing spirituality in our contemporary world.

In other local church communities the price tag attached to living the wisdom and social justice concerns of Jesus are too costly. They are too painful for those of us who are the powerful, living as the 'haves' of this world. Church people tend to be extremely generous with money and in supporting worthy humanitarian causes – and rightly so. However, real change will come about in the local, national and international communities when more followers of the Jesus Way live out their Christian discipleship alongside those who really hurt and suffer as a result of such as social exclusion and poverty.

To live the message of Jesus will cost us greatly. But the future of humankind may well depend upon all God's people, no matter by which gateway they have discovered the God-experience, living the wisdom of Isaiah 61. Even though it was the initial manifesto for the work and ministry of Jesus:

- To preach good news to the poor through our actions of social justice – and to use words if necessary…

- To proclaim freedom for the prisoners and recovery of sight for the blind, through our actions of social justice – and to use words if necessary…

• To release the oppressed, to proclaim the year of the Lord's favor through our actions of social justice – and to use words if necessary…

It is the way for all people of good will to live and to serve one another.

Appendix Seven

Matthew's Gospel has the disciples simply replying, "We have here only five loaves of bread and two fish."

In the later Gospel of Luke there is less sense of confrontation between the disciples and Jesus than in Mark's account, because they pragmatically replied, "If we are going to feed all these people, we will have to go and buy food."

But in John's Gospel things are entirely different. Here, John says that Jesus instigated this discussion by asking Philip, "Where will we get enough food to feed all these people?" According to John's version it is Philip who says to Jesus, "Don't you know that it would take almost a year's wages to buy only a little bread for each of these people?"

To compound these inconsistencies and contradictions in the stories, it is in John's Gospel alone that we are introduced to the young boy who has the five small loaves of barley bread and two fish.

Returning to Mark's version: Jesus persisted with his questioning. "How many loaves do you have? Go and see."

The disciples returned and said, "Five – and two fish."

So which Gospel account is the correct one? But then again, does it matter that there are such inconsistencies and contradictions? In my occasional discussions with those of a more literalist and fundamentalist Christian theology, it seems [a] not to matter even to them because they seem to ignore the inconsistencies and contradictions as though they do not exist, or [b] when pushed into responding, they bend over backwards and twist themselves inside out as they try to reconcile the differences.

I add that such inconsistencies and contradictions certainly do not matter to me. After all, these Scriptures were not written to be read as factual history. In the rabbinic Midrashic tradition, what is important is the underlying meaning and unity of the stories. As I understand this mythos story of the feeding of 5000, its meaning is not in the factual accuracy of what happened that late afternoon on the eastern shore of Lake Galilee, but the miracle is that people who were just like us, not yet fully human as the Spirit encourages us to be, shared the little that they had so that all had sufficient.

It was witnessing this for myself while working in Lithuania immediately after the fall of Communism that set me on a whole new discovery of Jesus. There I stood in amazement in the cold homes and frozen streets of January, seeing people who had very little sharing what they had with those who had even less. Here was the Christian Gospel being lived among people who had never heard the Christian Gospel!

Appendix Eight

A story of the two great banquets

Each banquet was held in neighboring halls. Both halls had a long table laden with all the finest food you could wish to see (just imagine a Methodist bring and share tea!). Both tables were lined with hundreds of people. The only problem was that the host of the banquets imposed the restriction that the food could only be taken from the tables by the use of 10 feet long chopsticks. After some hours the people in one banqueting hall were increasingly hungry and nothing had reached the mouths of the participants, but in the other hall the people were extremely well-fed and the table was empty. And the difference was simple. In the former hall the people tried to feed themselves but the chopsticks were so long they could not turn them to get the food to the mouth. In the latter hall the people simply shared by each person taking up some food in their chopsticks and reaching across the table to feed the person opposite them.

Now that is the real miracle of the story of the feeding of the 5000 – and it doesn't require us to abuse our intelligence or for us to suspend what we know to be true about science and the natural laws of the universe.

Appendix Nine

When considering the name Baal, what comes to mind? I suggest that usually it is the story of the conflict between Elijah, a prophet of the Hebrew God, and the prophets of Baal recorded in 1 Kings 18. But the history of the Hebrews long before the time of Elijah was entangled with worshippers of Baal. Even David while King (1000-961 BCE) took on and defeated followers of Baal [1 Chronicles 14]. 1 Kings 16 lists generations of Israel's kings who failed the Lord of Israel by worshipping Baal: Baasha; Zimri (although his reign lasted just seven days in 885 BCE); Omri, victor in a civil war for the throne (885-874 BCE); Ahab, son of Omri, who married Jezebel and even set up an altar for Baal (874-853 BCE). These were kings who led the people of Israel into sin in the eyes of the Lord.

In 2 Kings 10 there is an interesting story of subterfuge in which Jehu (841-814 BCE), worshipper of Israel's Lord, called all the Baal ministers to him for a promised grand sacrifice in the temple of Baal to 'honor' this false god. As soon as every minister of Baal was crowded into the temple, Jehu commenced the ceremony. He had new robes brought for the ministers and then he proceeded to make the burnt offering. At this point, when the ministers of Baal must have been feeling extremely glad and victorious, Jehu ordered his soldiers to go in and kill every one of them. After this slaughter Jehu had the 'sacred' stone brought out of the temple and destroyed it.

The people then destroyed the temple itself and the worship of Baal among Israel's people ceased – at least for a short time. By the time the writer of 2 Kings arrived at Chapter 17 the people of Israel were at it again – they cast two calf-shaped idols and built an Asherah pole. The people forgot about their own Lord and worshiped once again the gods of Baal. In 2 Kings 21 and 2 Chronicles 33 there is the story of the boy king, Manasseh, who went on to reign in Jerusalem for some 55 years, dying when he was 67 years old (696-642 BCE). Manasseh undid all the work of his father King Hezekiah and rebuilt altars to Baal and made an Asherah pole.

Manasseh's son Amon reigned for just two years (642-640 BCE) and he was no improvement on his father. But then Amon's son, Josiah, became King at the age of eight. He was well informed by advisers and he went on to order the removal of all items related to the worship of Baal from the Temple [2 Kings 23] and he restored the old ways including the Festival of the Passover. The prophet Jeremiah lamented the death in battle of Josiah but he continued to tackle those who worshipped Baal. There is more on the conflict between followers of the Hebrew Lord and worshippers of Baal in Psalms, Hosea and Zephaniah.

References

Churcher, J. (2009), *Setting Jesus Free*, O Books, Winchester, UK

Cornford, F.M. (1907), *Thucydides Mythistoricus*, Edward Arnold, London

Crossan, John Dominic (2007), *God and Empire*, Harper, San Francisco

Borg, Marcus, and Crossan, John Dominic (2008), *The Last Week*, SPCK, London

Crossan, John Dominic (2009), in *The Historical Jesus*, Ed. Beilby, J.K. & Eddy, P.R., IVP Academic, Downers Grove

Funk, Robert, et al (2002), *The Credible Jesus*, Polebridge, Santo Rosa

Goulder, Michael (1974), *Midrash and Lection in Matthew*, SPCK, London

Hengel, Martin (1977), *Crucifixion in the Ancient World and the Folly of the Message of the Cross*, Fortress, Philadelphia

Küng, Hans (1994), *Christianity*, Continuum, New York

Phillips, J.B. (1952), *Your God is Too Small*, Simon & Schuster, New York

Tillich, Paul (1963), *The Eternal Now*, Scribners, New York

West, Cornel (2008), *Hope on a Tightrope*, Smiley Books, New York

Also:

The New Jerome Biblical Commentary, (1989), Ed. Brown, Raymond E., Fitzmyer, Joseph A., Murphy, Roland E., Prentice Hall, New Jersey

The Amplified Bible, (1987), The Lockman Foundation

The Contemporary English Version (1995), American Bible Society

Questions For Group Discussion:
Written by Rev. Betty Saunders
'Dying to Live' Chapter One: Setting out on a Journey of Discovery

Relevance for ourselves is found in the story of the call of the fishermen and the extraordinary catch of fish by seeing it as a metaphor of the way in which we may experience the call to risk all to follow Jesus and find unexpected rewards – or as a metaphor of the way we may find the extraordinary in the ordinary. Share examples of occasions when you have been able to discover metaphorical truth within New Testament stories when you cease to worry about their historical truth. This is yet another time-honored way of approaching the Scriptures.

1] Four ways of reading the Gospels are suggested: at face value as a biographical story; as an expansion to the lectionary in Jewish Christian liturgy; as a myth-novel; as interpreted history. Which of these ways are new to you? Which ways would you like to explore further at this stage?

2] Wesley's quadrilateral of Scripture, Tradition, Reason and Experience are reinterpreted to take account of post-enlightenment thinking. Which of the quadrilateral have you most relied upon in your Christian life so far and which would you find most helpful in the light of this suggested reinterpretation?

3] The Student Christian Movement is an organization that has long advocated that Christians should read the Scriptures with the Bible in one hand and the newspaper in the other. That is the method demonstrated in this book in the choice of illustrations to show the present-day relevance of the stories of the Wise Men and the Slaughter of the Innocents. Suggest other present-day situations that illuminate the timeless myths of the Christmas stories.

4] Using a book of Gospel parallels, a Concordance or the footnotes in a good Study Bible, try looking up the alternative versions of the five stories quoted as the occasions where Jesus is identified as Son of God and note the differences.

'Dying to Live' Chapter Two: Mark's Gospel as Social Commentary

1] Mark is shown as protective of Peter's reputation. There seems to be evidence even in the differing Gospel accounts of very early disagreements between the followers of Jesus. Do you find this surprising, disturbing or reassuring?

2] Why do you think that the early church began to develop a hierarchy although the emphasis of Jesus was upon servant-hood? Are hierarchies and servant-hood incompatible? If not, what safeguards are needed?

a) "He who is not against us is for us" is recorded as a Jesus saying in Mark and Luke and the opposite only in Matthew's Gospel. Which statement seems to you to be most compatible with the way Jesus lived and what he taught? Think of incidents in the life and teaching of Jesus that illustrate one saying or the other.

b) How is this statement relevant for us today in relation to:
(i) people of other forms of the Christian faith different from our own?
(ii) those who follow other faiths?
(iii) people of different opinions, ways of life or cultures?

3] Think of ways in which we may need to accept change or break habits for the sake of love.

4] How would you reply to someone who sees the instructions quoted from Deuteronomy as a reason for seeing the Bible as an evil book and the God of the Bible as a cruel tyrant?

The following questions now relate to the chapters in the Gospel of Mark.

Mark Chapter 1

1] How do you respond to the assertion that his family may have rejected Jesus because he was becoming too interested in the spiritual that they considered him to be of no earthly use in the family business?

2] To what extent do you think the disciples developed their understanding (theology) of Jesus during those years together with Jesus, and how much did it develop in the decades after the execution of Jesus, with the benefit of hindsight?

3] Is there any place in this post-modern industrialized world for a theology of substitutionary atonement in which Jesus died specifically to save me from my sins? What are the alternative ways of understanding the life and execution of Jesus that may be more relevant to our contemporary world?

Mark Chapter 2

1] How do you understand 'spiritual healing'?

2] Share any experience you have of faith healing and your views about it, noting the way in which Jesus seems to attribute the healing to the faith of the person concerned, or the faith of his friends rather than attributing it to divine intervention.
In this chapter three incidents are listed where Jesus has to upset the

established order of things in order to fulfill his ministry. It is for the sake of his new vision of the Kingdom that the old order must change. The new wine requires new wineskins. Notice the characteristics of this new vision: forgiveness, healing, fellowship with outsiders, the primacy of human need over the petty application of rules.

3] To what extent do you think that one of the initial aims of Jesus was to seek a united and reformed Judaism – an aim that put him immediately on a collision course with the Pharisees and Sadducees?

Mark Chapter 3

1] Jesus developed a collaborative ministry. In what ways and to what extent can a minister in a church develop a collaborative ministry and why might it be important to work in this way?

2] If we understand that the choice of 12 as the number of designated apostles was a Midrash to relate it to the 12 tribes of Israel, does that make a difference to how we see their authority in the future church? Were they all of equal importance in the ensuing story? What about the women who followed Jesus? [Mark 5:40-41]

Mark Chapter 4

1] How does it change our understanding of the parable of the Sower if we recognize the link between Mark 4:12 and Isaiah 6:9-13?

2] Statistics about church attendance in the UK indicate a dying church. Why does it matter if the church dies?

3] Literalist preaching in some churches may account for the negative reaction of some of the population and their offer of certainty may attract some others but it does not account for the drift from all the churches that has been taking place during the last few generations. What changes are needed to make a difference? Is it only new wineskins that are needed or do we need new wine? – new structures, new music, new times and forms of worship or, in addition, a new and more open theology and the courage to explore and proclaim it?

Mark Chapter 5

1] What do the stories of the healing of the woman with the hemorrhage and the healing of Jairus' pubertal daughter say to us about the attitude of Jesus towards women and how this might affect issues of women in the church today?

2] Find other examples of the occasions when Jesus broke the barriers of his Society. What barriers does love require us to break in our day – into our personal lives and in our society?

Mark Chapter 6

1] What do you think were the reasons why the congregation at the Nazareth synagogue turned from acceptance to rejection? Can anything similar happen to a present-day leader – in the church or in politics?

2] Think of other references to the sea in the Old Testament and compare them with references to the sea in the literature of the UK, North America or in Greek mythology.

3] What other symbols of destructive power are most common in our fiction?

If we do not read the stories of the feeding of the 5000 and of the 4000 at their face value as miracle stories, what do you think is their significance?

Mark Chapter 7

1] "You have let go the commands of God and are holding on to the traditions of men." How do you apply this saying when you think about its application in the present day?

2] Do you consider the creeds and doctrines of the church as 'the commands of God' or as the 'traditions of men'? Do you find them a hindrance or a help in your faith? To what extent would your grown-up children give the same answer?

3] Read Isaiah 29:13-19. To what extent do you think that Jesus may be acting out the prophecy of Isaiah?

Mark Chapter 8

1] How do you interpret the story of the blind man? Read and compare the story of the healing of the man blind from birth, in John Chapter 9 and the conclusion in verses 39-41 and consider whether there may be an intended link between the physical blindness of the man and the spiritual blindness of the disciples [Mark 8:17- 21].

2] Who is Jesus for you? Has your understanding of Jesus changed or deepened with the years?

Mark Chapter 9

1] How do you interpret the cost of discipleship? The days of Roman persecution are over so what does this mean for present-day disciples? Why do you think that Jesus reacted so vehemently and called his friend the Devil?

2] How do you think that we should confront wrongdoing if we are following the Jesus way?

3] Who are the powerless in our society as children were in the time of Jesus?

4] Have you ever felt that you would like to 'hang a millstone around the neck' of some wrongdoer in the news or within your experience?

Mark Chapter 10

1] How do you understand the teaching of Jesus about marriage and divorce in the light of the patriarchal property-based nature of marriage at the time? What does the teaching of Jesus about the two becoming one imply about his view of the essential meaning of marriage?

2] The two sons of Zebedee and that of Bartimaeus both make requests. Notice the differences. What would you like to demand of God?

3] If you do not believe in an interventionist God how do you deal with intercessory prayer?

Mark Chapter 11

1] We have all heard the story of Palm Sunday many times and listened to many interpretations. How do you imagine it and what is your understanding of its significance?

2] Consider the interpretation of the story of the barren fig tree as a parable for the barren state of the Temple in its failure to produce the fruit of mercy and justice that God requires.

3] Read Jeremiah 7:1-15. What relevance does this story have for the churches today?

Mark Chapter 12

1] "Do all the good you can by all the means you can." Most of us do not have many ways of combating social evils on a large scale although we may use what power we have as citizens and consumers and in the formation of public opinion. How else may we 'cross boundaries'? What are the divisions in our society?

2] What might it mean to see the message of the resurrection as primarily a message for the present rather than a belief about the past and the future?

Mark Chapter 13

The Signs of the Times

1] Jesus, like Jeremiah and the other prophets before him was interpreting the political events of his time and knew what would happen if the Jews revolted against Roman occupation – just as surely as the owner would expect the fig tree to respond to the changes of the season. What should people do when a cruel government is in power? Collaborate? Revolt? Wait for a Messiah – a strong leader? Endure peacefully? It is a perennial problem in history and in current events.

2] How do you interpret the 'signs of the times' when you consider the decline of the Christian churches in Western Europe and their growth in Asia and Africa?

Mark Chapter 14

1] The stories told in this chapter form a simple human drama that does not lose its power however often we hear it. The variations in the accounts given in the different Gospels need to be acknowledged. Does this trouble you or do you find it helpful to understand some of the processes and time lapses involved in their composition?

2] Do you find it helpful to know the reference to Amos 2:16 in the story of the young man who ran away naked?

3] What do you think was the motivation of Judas?

Mark Chapters 15 and 16

There is a great deal in the world to discourage and depress us. Identify those things that you see as signs of hope and joy and new life.